PRAISE FOR
WHO'S IN THE WAITING ROOM?

"I had the opportunity to work with Neal as a psychotherapist many years ago. Neal's book is a brave, vulnerable, authentic sharing of a very deprived, difficult, and painful childhood. Yet, through sheer resilience, intelligence, and perseverance, Neal managed to survive and find love and success in his adult life. The book is aimed at young people facing extraordinary adversity and struggling to find a path to move forward in their lives. What is unique about this book is that while telling his deeply moving story, he also provides hope and tools to navigate through it. A truly inspiring book!"

ELLEN MARCH FEINSTEIN
LCSW, Clinical Social Worker, New York City

"Neal Goldstein is a lawyer's lawyer. He has been a wonderful mentor to me and hundreds of other lawyers across the country. In his book, Neal captures that shared wisdom in his stories about his challenging life and successful career. Every new lawyer should read this book!"

JIM HACKING *Cohost of the Maximum Lawyer Podcast and Immigration Lawyer*

"Far from just writing another self-help book, Neal Goldstein takes us into a world of despair and confusion and shows us what it takes to come out the other side. I found my heart breaking for the young boy abandoned by family and thrown unprepared into the caretaker role, only to catch myself later applauding and celebrating the thoughtful, caring, and strong man who had emerged. By weaving deeply personal and relatable stories together with general principles for success and happiness, Neal provides the reader with a strong foundation for growth that we all can relate to and, more importantly, that we can all learn from."

ARNIE PREMINGER *Founder and CEO, Sunrise Association: international summer and year-round programs for children with cancer and their siblings*

"Neal Goldstein is one of the most thoughtful, genuine lawyers. He has spent his career connecting with clients, colleagues, and opposing counsel to build a personal and professional network that is truly awe-inspiring. Neal's book shares his insight into creating deeply personal and professional connections that have led to a rich and fulfilling career. Neal is a treasure, and the read is a joy."

SETH PRICE, ESQ. *Managing Partner, Price Benowitz; Founder and CEO, Blue Shark Digital; Washington, DC*

"I was sitting in a room full of young, old, and eager lawyers, all trying to find their way through the business aspect of their law firms. We went around the room telling our stories and how we got here. Finally, it was Neal's turn to address the room. A visibly nervous man stood up and started to make remarks about his childhood. All eyes and ears were on him. Nobody moved or made a sound. He described having to leave high school to take care of his mother and family. What I heard was the most humble, honest, and self-reflective story. I simply cannot describe what was going through my mind, hearing such a tremendous story and knowing the endurance, humility, and determination it must have taken to get to where Neal is today. This surreal moment changed my thinking and humbled me to no end. We immediately struck up a personal relationship. Once again, I am so humbled by reading Neal's new book. It is a true story of a real man that we all aspire to be. This is a book and story you must have your children read—a true lesson on a life that will effect change in your life."

HARLAN SCHILLINGER *Legal Marketing Expert*

"Wow! This book is for anyone who feels like they've tried everything to succeed, but something is still missing. Neal Goldstein shortens the 'wisdom learning curve' by sharing his story with courage, warmth, and vulnerability. Reading this book validated my experiences in life and gave me hope for the future. Highly recommend!"

JENNIFER QUINN ("JENNYQ") *CMO, Strategist, and Author*

"Neal's story of resilience is as enlightening as it is inspiring. The lessons he shares in this book are valuable to anyone seeking to achieve meaningful and lasting success."

MICHAEL MOGILL *Founder and CEO of Crisp*

"It's no surprise that this book, at its core, is about relationships. I've known Neal for many years, and the gift of this book is that, through the stories of his life, he is able to help others through his compassion and wisdom. His counsel and suggestions ask the reader to look within themselves to build on old relationships and create new ones. This book will help people take the necessary steps to have more successful business and personal lives."

ERNEST MINGIONE *Actor and Lawyer*

"Our ability to connect with others is the ultimate measure of our success. Building authentic and meaningful connections—that's Neal's passion. This is what he does so well. Neal and I are both lawyers. We share the same last name but are not related. Other than that, we are both humans trying to make the world a better place. I met Neal at a professional event and instantly knew that he and I would stay in touch and be friends for life. This ability to connect is Neal's gift. I knew that Neal had a tough time growing up. But the early pages of this book are genuinely heartbreaking. All children deserve to feel loved, nurtured, and safe. From this troubled upbringing, Neal found his calling and developed. Instead of becoming bitter, he developed a warmth, grace, and humility that makes him easy to connect with. Neal's journey, in this book, is indispensable for anyone looking to understand how to build relationships—real human connections."

JOSHUA GOLDSTEIN *Goldstein Immigration Lawyers, Los Angeles*

"I have known Neal for my entire adult business life. My relationship with Neal has changed the course of my journey, and I find it difficult to think about where I would be today without him. However, reading his book has provided me with insights that I never knew, things to think about (especially about myself) that I would not have thought about, and pure hope and joy about life. Life is truly a journey about learning, and Neal's message finds a way to guide us all to have a better life. One thing that stands out to me is the timelessness of Neal's message. In today's online world, with such 'connectivity,' it is amazing how many people feel disconnected. The facade of social media hides more profound challenges for people, even you or me—challenges no different than what Neal has traveled through.

"Thank you to Neal for bringing this to light—for truly, it is not about what you know, but who you know and how you relate in the world!"

BRIAN MITTMAN, ESQ. *The Disability Guys*

"Neal tells wonderful stories about his life and the lessons of genuine human relationships to live well."

DAVID MEERMAN SCOTT *Author of twelve books including* **Fanocracy**, *a* **Wall Street Journal** *bestseller*

"Once you look inside Neal's life story, you will see a man who has overcome enormous obstacles and struggles—stories of hardship that would tempt most to quit. Neal's life story is a testament to his courage and resilience. Everyone should read this book."

JOHN H. FISHER *Author of* **The Power of a System** *and* **The Law Firm of Your Dreams**

"Neal Goldstein writes about his life with true candor and insight, becoming a guide readers can trust as they explore how their own experiences and relationships have shaped who they are and who they'd like to become. *Who's in the Waiting Room?* is a generous gift."

ONA GRITZ *Author, most recently, of* **Present Imperfect: Essays**

"When reading through Neal's book, what jumps out is that the life stories that he has shared inspire compassion, caring, and the promise of a better future. The book is motivating and uplifting with the hope of a better future for all of us."

PAULA CIALELLA *Attorney, New Castle, Pennsylvania*

"It is a rare combination to find a book that melds genuine relationship building together with actions that we all know but often become complacent about. Since speaking with Neal over the years, I began to see challenges in life differently and began prioritizing my relationships because, in the long run, that is all that matters."

GURPREET "SONNY" SINGH
Commercial Real Estate Broker, Floral Park, New York

"Some of us may grow up feeling alone, but we're never alone in life. Sometimes in order to realize this, we need a new way of looking at things. We need someone to give us a better lens to look through to help us interpret what's happened to us and what our options are moving forward.

"That's precisely what Neal does in this book. He takes you by the hand, lets you know it's OK, and shows you a new and better way to approach your life. At the end of each chapter, the short and action-able thought-provoking steps will help you pull everything together and move forward instead of remaining in the past. This book is a gift. Thank you, Neal."

MITCH JACKSON *2013 California Litigation Lawyer of the Year*

"I have been an attorney for the past thirty years, and out of hundreds of lawyers I've met, Neal stands out as one who is true and genuine. Neal's book is about building success through genuine and authentic relationships. His ability to guide the reader through his success tips is key to understanding how to connect even more deeply with others, both on a business and personal level."

MICHAEL SAMUEL *The Samuel Law Firm, New York City*

"When reading Neal's book, you immediately feel a connection through his stories. They are told with a sense of genuineness and authenticity that you can't help but take away some of your own lessons. His passion for being fully present and in the moment, especially with his family, is truly inspiring."

CHRISTOPHER NICOLAYSEN *Springs Law Group, Colorado Springs, Colorado*

WHO'S
in the
WAITING
ROOM?™

NEAL GOLDSTEIN

WHO'S
in the
WAITING
ROOM?™

**CREATE THE LIFE YOU WANT THROUGH THE
POWER OF AUTHENTIC RELATIONSHIPS**

Advantage.

Published by Advantage, Charleston, South Carolina.
Member of Advantage Media.

ADVANTAGE is a registered trademark, and the Advantage colophon is a trademark of Advantage Media Group, Inc.

Printed in the United States of America.

10 9 8 7 6 5 4 3 2 1

ISBN: 978-1-64225-540-9 (Hardcover)
ISBN: 979-8-89188-201-0 (Paperback)
ISBN: 978-1-64225-539-3 (eBook)

LCCN: 2022910912

Cover design by Megan Elger.
Layout design by Amanda Haskin.

This publication is designed to provide accurate and authoritative information in regard to the subject matter covered. It is sold with the understanding that the publisher is not engaged in rendering legal, accounting, or other professional services. If legal advice or other expert assistance is required, the services of a competent professional person should be sought.

Advantage Media helps busy entrepreneurs, CEOs, and leaders write and publish a book to grow their business and become the authority in their field. Advantage authors comprise an exclusive community of industry professionals, idea-makers, and thought leaders. Do you have a book idea or manuscript for consideration? We would love to hear from you at **AdvantageMedia.com**.

**To my mom, Shirley Baum,
and my grandmother, Fannie Baum.**

*"To every thing there is a season, and a time to every purpose
under the heaven: A time to weep, and a time to laugh; a
time to mourn, and a time to dance."*
Ecclesiastes 3:1-8 King Solomon

CONTENTS

PRAISE FOR I

FOREWORD XVII

INTRODUCTION 1

CHAPTER 1 5

Growing Up Alone

CHAPTER 2 23

Finding Your People

CHAPTER 3 39

Most Great Moments Involve Others

CHAPTER 4 57

Listen More Than You Talk

CHAPTER 5 83

Face-to-Face Contact

CHAPTER 6. 97

Building Bridges

CHAPTER 7. 115

Share Your Story

CONCLUSION 129

LET'S CONNECT 135

ACKNOWLEDGMENTS 137

ABOUT THE AUTHOR 141

FOREWORD

What are the stories that I find most grounding and full of connection? More often than not, the stories touch on vulnerability and the traits that make us truly human. It is where these moments come from as they become unearthed through explorations of our relationships through richness and depth.

That's why I'm thrilled to be introducing Neal Goldstein's book *Who's in the Waiting Room? Create the Life You Want through the Power of Authentic Relationships.* His book is exactly that, a forensic, beautiful, deep dive into some of his relationships, with the initial intention of sharing his story with his children and guiding them through their relationship-building. But what Neal has also gone on to create is a practical and emotive testimony to the power of relationships and building connections with others that everyone can apply.

Neal's incredible success as a lawyer puts him in a fantastic position as an authoritative storyteller with tangible examples and experience in forging long-lasting connections with others to generate results. His lived experience and personal history provide readers with insight into how these connections shaped him and how he used them as a bedrock for his success—how to connect, how to survive, how to lead, and how to excel. The complexity in our own stories can be a source of knowledge, and we can use them to learn prevailing lessons about relationships.

Whether you're looking to change your career path, launch a new business, network at your next event, or feel closer to those around you, this book encourages you to embrace today's ability to nurture your relationships. Because we all need relationships, and we all need human connection, especially in trying times and moments.

This book serves as a timely reminder of how meaningful relationships take time but are one of the most worthwhile investments we can make. And if we learn how to listen to others, it's one of our most impactful and authentic forms of connection. If people feel listened to, amazing things can happen.

In an ever-polarizing world, with social media often substituting for real-life connections, it's never been more important to find common ground with others. Neal and I share many similar thoughts on this, and there are many crossovers with the human-to-human (H2H) approach.

This book is for anyone willing to connect at a deeper level with others and learn from each other, helping to bridge divides and taking control of the building and rebuilding of relationships.

There is no better time to take this book and savor every detail as we navigate our way out of two years of pandemic life, when our ability to build relationships has been tested and knocked for six. What jumps out is the necessity to revitalize our ability to make face-to-face connections.

Neal poses searching questions that challenge us to do this and gives actionable tips to open ourselves up to new opportunities and ease back into our power to connect with others. Some of the challenges might feel difficult—and I love this book because Neal shares his personal history so generously and with such humility that it urges you to pause and reflect on your own life and relationships.

Neal's openness to share his story makes this book stay with us long after finishing the final page. More importantly, it's impossible not to acknowledge that sharing your own unique story with others is one of the most powerful things you can do to create connections and show what makes you human.

BRYAN KRAMER *Executive Coach and Mentor, H2H Companies*

INTRODUCTION

When I began writing this book, my original plan was to create something solely for my kids—something to leave them as part of my legacy. But as I put words to paper, I realized that there might be something in my story that could help others, maybe people who didn't have the ideal life growing up but who are looking for ways to turn that around.

It all started following the loss of two people very important to me: my mother and my grandmother. After their deaths, I was left with a lot of jewelry, furniture, and clothing that I didn't really need. Among all the items left for me to sift through were pictures, which meant so much to me but often raised more questions than answers. Why was my mother smiling in this one? Why was my grandmother not smiling in that one? What was on my mother's mind in this picture with my brothers and me? Pictures allow you to remember a face, a time, and a place. What they can never do is allow you to know what someone was feeling at a given moment.

I wanted to change that for my kids. I didn't want them wondering, so I decided to write down my story. I wanted them to step back in time and journey with me through my early years when I was adrift so that, hopefully, as they confront obstacles and challenges in life, they may have a road map or guide to help them. Because, as we all know, life will come knocking at the door, and you can't walk away from it. You can't close the drapes and hide behind the couch. You have to answer that door. And you need to be ready for what's on the other side.

For most people, that knock comes later in life. But for me, that knock came very early—and often.

That's why I decided that this could be a book not just for my kids but maybe for other kids whose parents are absent or don't offer them the guidance they need—really for anyone who's facing extraordinary adversity.

In my law practice, I've represented thousands of clients who have overcome great challenges. And what I've seen in so many of them is one common factor—the relationships that they have in their lives. Not just acquaintances or Facebook friends but authentic and loving relationships. I'm talking about the kind of people who you can call on, those who are going to be honest with you, who will be there for you, who will take the journey with you, wherever that journey goes.

Genuine relationships make all the difference between success or failure. So often I've seen ambitious people dream of building a successful business and creating a vibrant community of clients and colleagues but then be persuaded by hurdles and challenges that those things are inaccessible. But in the chapters ahead, I will share with you how relationships in all areas of our lives can help overcome those challenges and lead to success.

GENUINE RELATIONSHIPS MAKE ALL THE DIFFERENCE BETWEEN SUCCESS OR FAILURE.

What I've seen through my own journey is that those relationships don't even need to be for a lifetime. Even momentary relationships can help you navigate the obstacles along the way. We're not created to be in this world alone. If you think that you can resolve life's major issues and challenges by yourself, trust me, that doesn't always work. While self-reliance and self-confidence are needed to succeed in this world, that doesn't mean you have to be alone on life's journey.

Today, my success as a lawyer has not only afforded me the life I could have only dreamed of as a teenager but also, more importantly, has left an indelible mark on so many of the clients whom I've represented. Clients whom I was blessed to have retained me and allowed me to assist in help putting their lives back together; many of whom I consider my friends and who have invited me into their lives even after our attorney-client relationship ceased. In the more than thirty years that I've been in practice, I've never had a client ask me how many million-dollar verdicts I have won. That's not what they want to hear. They're more interested in the pictures of my kids and me on the wall. They're more interested in sitting down with me over a cup of coffee than they are about being in my fancy office.

As you will read, where I am today is miles from the world I grew up in. But through all the caregiving for a mother too sick to care for me, abuse and abandonment by my father, dropping out of high school, and going hungry more often than I care to remember, there was a crushing loneliness—the kind of loneliness that comes from lacking the relationships you need when all else is failing. Having discovered my own path to success, in the pages ahead, I'm going to share what I've learned along the way.

In my life, the number one most powerful, most transformative force has been other people. And so this is a book about relationships—why they matter and how to build them. In the pages ahead, you'll discover the five behaviors you can adopt to foster quality relationships: finding your people, acknowledging the need for each other, listening more than you talk, recognizing the value of face-to-face contact, and finding common ground.

As I write these words, we're exiting a pandemic that has engulfed the world, and if there was ever a moment to take a breather and look at our lives, it is now. As you read through this book, consider your own "waiting room" and what that means for you and, more importantly, who will occupy that space. After reading it, I hope you will find that you are open to creating new relationships and building on existing ones.

In writing this book, I discovered that pausing to take an inventory of your life relationships and how they have shaped who you are today is a great way to learn more about yourself—more than you ever imagined possible.

To help you do the same with your life, I've included at the end of each chapter a list of actionable success moves that encourage you to recall your life's experiences and use what you discover about yourself and others to create better relationships. You may also want to keep your notes in a journal, which will allow you to refer back to and build on them as you progress through the chapters and gain more understanding about the importance of having others in your life.

CHAPTER 1

GROWING UP ALONE
WITHOUT PRACTICAL PARENTAL GUIDANCE, WHERE DO YOU START?

*A successful man is one who can lay a firm foundation
with the bricks others have thrown at him.*
—DAVID BRINKLEY

On a beautiful summer morning in 1989, I drove to my mother's two-bedroom apartment. Driving through my hometown, Far Rockaway, New York, a rush of memories flowed through me. Seeing the Green Line and Jamaica Line buses on Seagirt Boulevard, the major thoroughfare in the neighborhood, reminded me of all the bus rides to school and work. Passing by the stores at ground level in the building where my mother lived reminded me of the times my brother and I would grab a slice of pizza. I was anxious and hopeful because this was a day like no other.

My mother lived on the twenty-fifth floor of what, a decade earlier when she moved in, was considered to be a very nice apartment building alongside Far Rockaway Beach. As the elevator slowly climbed floor by floor, my anticipation grew—I couldn't wait to see her. The doors opened on the twenty-fifth floor, and I walked to the apartment at the end of the hall where my mother lived. The door was painted red, like all the others, and there was a mezuzah on the right doorpost. In mainstream Judaism, a mezuzah is affixed to the doorpost of Jewish homes to fulfill the biblical commandment to "write the words of God on the gates and doorposts of your house." In Talmudic times, the mezuzah was also valued for its protective powers—it was posted to ward off evil spirits.

With sweaty hands, I opened the door and was met by my mom's healthcare aide and friend, Lucille, who said, "Mom's in the bedroom." No surprise, since, by that point in time, my mother was spending most of her days and nights in her bedroom.

But today was a very special day, so when I walked into her bedroom, it was a little different from my normal visits. She was sitting up in her wheelchair wearing a beautiful white dress with a red floral pattern—and a beaming smile. She, too, was filled with anticipation—and pride. "Are you ready?" I asked.

"I'm ready," she replied, with the biggest smile I'd seen on her face in a long time.

I helped my mother to the car, and we headed to our destination. My mother loved being the passenger in the car and I loved driving, so we were a good team. As we drove along with the car windows open, the salty smell of the ocean air gave me a moment of real happiness. Growing up by the beach was wonderful; maybe it's the constant smell of summer, but living by the ocean gets in your blood, and it's very hard to get it out. In fact, I live by the beach today. But driving along with my mother that day, the smell flooded my mind with good memories, crowding out the bad ones that would have otherwise filled my head from being so close to the place where I grew up.

We stopped on the way to our destination, New York City, to pick up my brother Cary. With him on board, it was an hour-long journey filled with laughter and happiness.

But it wasn't always that way.

I was born in Brooklyn's Carson Peck Memorial hospital, a place that was demolished in 2003. My mother's doctor was there because she had just moved from Brooklyn to Far Rockaway. My parents had moved to a huge apartment development called Wavecrest Gardens, which was nestled at the eastern end of the Rockaway Peninsula. Looking at it today, it seems like a huge cluster of red brick, six-story apartment buildings. Many areas of the development were formed in groups of six buildings, each with a common area that was paved with cement walks filled with trees, bushes, grassy areas, and benches. People used to congregate on these terraces, as the residents called them: Older people sat on their chairs, kids played, and others just walked around. These were magical places, particularly in the summer. Our terrace gave us a front seat to the fireworks on the Fourth of July and the parties that the adults often threw on Labor Day.

We hung out at the terrace when it was too cold to go to the beach; otherwise, that's where you could find us. Within five minutes of leaving the building we lived in, we could be walking on the beach with sand between our toes. Everyone went there and to the boardwalk, which ran parallel to the beach. No camps, summer homes, or extended vacations for the people who lived in my neighborhood. Where we lived was our summer home—year-round. It was glorious.

My family lived in a two-bedroom apartment with an eat-in kitchen, small dining area, living room, and one bathroom. We had a kitchen table and a dining room table, which back then was referred to as a dinette. Living room furnishings included a sleeper sofa, a green barrel chair, and a red love seat. There was also a desk in the living room, which always seemed a little out of place, and we had a set of red encyclopedias and the World Book, which my mother purchased every year from a door-to-door salesman. I think she felt that the desk and books promoted good study habits; she loved books and always told me, "Don't ever throw them away."

Along with my mother and father, I lived with my two older brothers, Sheldon and Cary. Sheldon was my oldest brother, and he and Cary were born three years apart. I came along five years after Cary. Planned? I don't think so. Initially the three of us shared one bedroom. Cary and I slept in bunk beds, and I was always on the bottom bunk. When Sheldon left the house to live at school, that left just Cary and me to share the bedroom.

Although Cary was only five years older than me, it felt more like twenty, and he and Sheldon were complete opposites. Sheldon was about six feet tall, dark haired, slender, wore black glasses, and always seemed kind of nerdy. Cary was the epitome of cool: good looking, with a head full of curly brown hair that, when left unbrushed, could make him look like a lion. He could act like a tough guy (as a kid and a young adult, I always thought that was cool) and at the same time be the nice kid who everyone liked. In high school, he was intelligent, charismatic, and a real charmer with the girls.

Initially, Sheldon and I were closer. He always engaged me in kid games, like "army men" with those green plastic soldiers, and sometimes we had toy guns that we played with outside. Cary didn't seem to want to know me. Other than the hell-on-earth teasing he dished out—which often resulted in a "stop teasing your brother" warning from my mom—Cary barely looked at me. More on that in a later chapter.

While Sheldon initially went to public school, he entered full-time religious school at an early age at the encouragement of my grandmother. He remained a good person, but over time his behavior became increasingly odd, and he detached himself from his friends—and later on in life, from our family. So while he had been there for me when I was very young, he left very early on and has been absent for most of my life.

My father was tall, broad shouldered, and bald. I never saw him as a classy guy (honestly, how many kids think their parents are classy?). In fact, I always saw him as pretty ignorant. He had a heavy footstep and a rough Brooklyn tough-guy image. He was a salesman for a jewelry business in Brooklyn and sold goods through his own business connections, not at the company headquarters. He used the bedroom he shared with my mother as his base of operations. I remember seeing brand-new watches in their velvet-lined boxes laying out in a row on the bed, along with his paperwork. I have to admit that he was a very good salesman. He shook hands with everyone he met, tried to speak Spanish to potential Hispanic clients, and was well liked and considered a nice guy by people who didn't know him as I did. People actually wanted to do business with him.

At home, however, I saw a different side of him. He often lost his patience and always seemed angry. He had no trouble hitting us with his hands and sometimes with a belt.

Yet I would be disingenuous if I didn't say there were a few good moments with him. He often took me with him to get ice cream. He liked to drive his car, and when I was very young, I remember riding in it with him when he took me to work, or to see his parents, or even to his fraternal lodge for holiday parties. We went to the beach a few times, and he used his big hands to smear suntan lotion on my face, and then we would walk on the sand with him wearing big black sandals and, get ready for it, black socks. Those are really the only moments of caring that I remember about him.

Meanwhile, my mother's overwhelming health problems overshadowed every ounce of care she was able to give or any level of control she felt she might have had in her role as a mother. She was never physically affectionate, but I always knew she loved me—she always had my best interests at heart, and I knew she would do anything for me, if she could. In fact, she always proclaimed how much she loved being a mother, and she had a contagious laugh, which I still remember today.

But I never remember a time when she did not have trouble walking. She was born in 1928 in Brooklyn and was often doted on by her parents (my grandparents), so I've heard. She shared with me that her early life, before she became ill, was great. She grew up in the East New York section of Brooklyn with her aunts, uncles, and cousins either living on the same block or a stone's throw away from her apartment building.

From pictures I've seen of my mother, she was a beautiful child, with blond hair that turned brown when she was in her teens. She was around five feet tall, slender, and always fashionably dressed. Her long hair was always perfectly coiffed, as if she was ready to enter a beauty pageant at any moment. She seemed to have a lot of friends and was always traveling and taking pictures. Indeed, my mother and the camera seemed to have a mutual love affair!

When she was in her early twenties, she was running around on the roof of her building when she suddenly went blind—and stayed blind for three days. The doctors didn't know what was wrong with her, so they sent her to an ophthalmologist who was able to identify the problem—she had multiple sclerosis (MS). MS affects the central nervous system by destroying the myelin sheath covering the nerves and disrupting the messages from the brain to different parts of the body. Often, it affects the lower and upper extremities and then works its way around the body in a very disastrous manner.

Back in the 1940s, when she was diagnosed, there weren't a lot of options for treatment, but fortunately, she went into remission, a stage that lasted a good twenty years. She gave birth to my two brothers but was told not to have another child because the stress it would place on her body could trigger the MS. Then, five years later, I came along, and sure enough, her MS began to slowly creep back into her life. Fortunately for me, the one time she rebelled in her life worked in my favor—but not in hers. Talk about self-sacrifice.

Because of her illness, my memories of good moments with my mother mostly happened when I was very young or much later in life. The years in between were filled more with life lessons than with fun and laughter. I remember her reading books with me as we sat on the red love seat in the living room. I remember going with her to the local supermarket and taking pickles out of the barrel. I remember her cooking, which looking back, I realize wasn't very good, but what did I know as a kid? She was no Julia Child, but I loved it, especially when she made red Jell-O and all kinds of pudding. She also made a dish on Sundays that had cut-up hot dogs, onions, and beans. She clearly did not inherit, nor did she have any interest in taking up, my grandmother's fabulous cooking.

When I was about five years old, my mother walked with a limp and used a baby carriage as a walking aid. Whether it was me or groceries, she used the carriage to haul things around when her legs and balance were too weak for her to carry anything. The carriage more or less masked her walking issues.

My mother's worsening illness slowly took its toll on her ability to walk and grasp items in her hands. Before I was ten, she started randomly falling. She might be returning home after a stop at the food store and would fall on her way back to the building. In those early days of the illness, she was able to get back up by crawling to a fence or handrail and slowly pulling herself up until she had a better footing. I would watch and wait and then we would continue walking. When at home, I'd be in the living room, hear a crash in the kitchen, and go in to find her crying over a broken glass on the floor. I'd seen her crying when she was cutting onions, but this was different. But when I'd ask what was wrong, she would just reply, "Oh, nothing; everything is okay" or "I just accidentally dropped the glass." Over time, those accidents became more frequent.

Those moments made me feel scared and lonely: scared because I didn't know what was going on, since no one ever sat me down and told me what was happening to my mom, and lonely because I had nobody to talk to about what was going on. I had no close relationships in my family or otherwise at that time.

Over time, the carriage was no longer sufficient as a walking aid, and she started using a walker, a four-legged aluminum frame with rubber feet. Although it clearly helped her, it was a problem for me because it so clearly showed that she was someone who had trouble walking. I was embarrassed when my mother would attempt to walk outside or come downstairs to the terrace while I was there playing with some kids. For me, that walker was a flashing sign saying, "Hey, look at the kid with his crippled mother." Often, when she tried to walk outside, she would fall, and the neighbors would have to help pick her up off the ground. When I was young, I tried to look away or walk away from the situation.

When I was about eleven, my mother's illness accelerated. Even with the aid of the walker, she began falling more and more and started to lose control of her urinary and bowel functions. Often, when I came home, I would find the police in the apartment. When my mother fell, she would crawl to the phone and then call them for help. She began to require more assistance with personal needs, including in the bathroom. Sheldon was out of the house by that time, Cary was never at home, and my father was often gone on business (or simply didn't seem to care—more on that in a moment), so it was up to me to help my mother. There I was, not even a teen yet, and I had to help my mom with things I would never want my own son to do for me today.

It was around that time when the early morning fights between my mom and dad began, and I even remember my father making fun of my mother for her inability to control her bladder. Of course, that often led to my mother crying, and finally, she voluntarily gave up the marital bed and began sleeping on our pullout sofa in the living room. Normally, that bed was reserved for my oldest brother on his rare visits home or for my grandmother when she would come to help my mother. In those days, Cary was usually sleeping over at a friend's house, so I was the only one home who would help my mother because my father never did.

One morning, I heard a big thump, and I ran to the living room to see my mother lying on the bare wooden floor, crying and bleeding from her head. She had fallen trying to get out of bed and start her day. Instinctively, I quickly grabbed a washcloth and held it against her head to help control the blood. My father, leaving to start his workday, walked right by us without saying anything. No helping hand, no words, not even a sideways glance of sympathy. His coldness was unimaginable then, and it left an indelible imprint on my psyche—to this day, I believe that one act changed me forever.

Even at that young age, taking care of my mother and with no one around to help, I used to wonder, "What's going to happen to me? Where am I going to go? What happens to me if Mom is no longer here?" Inwardly, I was definitely an angry kid on some level, although it really never manifested itself outwardly—I was actually a shy kid who didn't know how to relate to other people very well. The few incidents that did occur were the result of my loneliness, which is a cousin of anger, which is a cousin of depression.

A big part of the problem was that I just didn't know what was going on because no one ever sat me down and told me, "Your mother has MS, and this is what that means, and this is what's going to happen." One time when I acted up in third grade, the teacher said to me, "I wish I could slap your face." But the few times I was sent to the principal's office, I would overhear him saying to colleagues, "We can't call his mother; she's not well." It seemed like everyone knew more about my mother's health than me.

Nighttime was particularly difficult because I was often left alone with my mother. Cary would stay out late and often slept at friends' homes. My father increasingly didn't come home, so living in apartment 6A became an unsettling place, especially after dark. At that age, a child just wants to feel safe. With Sheldon off to school and Cary always out doing something with his friends, I was alone in the bedroom and often had trouble going to sleep at night. Living on the top floor, I could sometimes hear people walking around on the roof of the building. Even riding up and down the elevator to get to and from our apartment was extremely scary. It was old and noisy, and riding in it all alone, my imagination often threatened to get the best of me: What happens if it stops? What happens if it doesn't stop and keeps going right through the roof? What happens if it suddenly lets go and plummets to the ground? I can laugh about those fears today, but back then, they just intensified the anxiety and loneliness I felt.

As my mother's condition worsened, the arguing between my parents increased. One New Year's Eve, my mother was invited to celebrate at a neighbor's party. Wanting some sense of normalcy in her life, she asked my father if he wanted to go over with her, but he snapped back that he wasn't interested. Instead, he went out somewhere, and she ended up staying home with me. Then there was the time my father wanted to go out for Chinese food. I was excited that we were getting out, and even my mother decided to go. With her walker, she slowly made her way to the elevator, and we took it to the basement where the car was parked. My father made his way to the garage entry door, where he waited while my mother shuffled from the elevator. But he quickly grew impatient and announced, "I'm not waiting." He told me to come with him, and my mother, probably sensing my desire to finally be getting out and doing something, told me to go ahead. We drove away and left her standing there to make her way back up the elevator on her own—more alone time for my mother and more guilt for me to digest for the next few decades.

I don't recall my father ever saying anything supportive to my mother, laughing with her, buying her personal gifts, or even hugging her or holding her hand in her darkest days. In fact, he continued to mock her incontinence and "accidents," and because she was no longer able to perform her marital obligations, he began increasingly staying out late at night or not coming home at all, as I mentioned earlier. Through the wall in my bedroom closet, I could overhear his conversations, including one where he was talking with a friend about going to X-rated films. Even then, at age eleven, I knew something wasn't quite right.

Ultimately, my mother's illness progressed to the point that she needed a wheelchair to get around. We could not afford one, so my Grandma Fannie obtained one from her nephew, who was a doctor on

Long Island. I vividly recall the day my father first saw the wheelchair in the living room, folded and leaning against the wall. You could tell by the stride of his black dress shoes against the wooden floor that he had something to say, and it wasn't going to be good. "Who paid for this?" he barked. "Where did you get this from?" My mother told him that my grandmother had made the arrangements and that there was no cost to him. He then escaped to his bedroom without any further comment.

ANGELS DO EXIST—GRANDMA FANNIE

Some angels don't have wings, so the saying goes, but everyone needs their own angel on earth. Someone who just wants you to be happy and will do all they can to help you through the challenges in your life. For me, that was Grandma Fannie.

Born in 1902 in Tyszowce (Tishovitz), in southeast Poland, she was one of nine children of parents Cora and Samuel. She and some of her siblings came to America with thousands of other Jewish refugees fleeing oppression and religious persecution. They joined her father in Brooklyn while her mother and the rest of her siblings remained in Poland—three of her siblings were ultimately killed in the Holocaust.

Grandma Fannie met my Grandpa Nathan in Brooklyn, and they married on July 10, 1927. Both worked in the growing garment industry: Grandma as a seamstress, Grandpa as a tailor. After my mother was born in 1928, they opened a candy and soda shop, Baum's, on Pitkin Avenue, which had a long lunch counter and sold egg creams. My mother was an only child, but because my grandparents were both from close-knit families, they lived within walking distance of many relatives.

When my mom brought my father home to meet her parents, they didn't have a good feeling about him. Still, they gave my mother a beautiful wedding and a somewhat lavish one from the photos I've seen.

My grandfather was diagnosed with colon cancer and passed away at the relatively young age of fifty-eight, so he had been gone for several years when my father walked out. Almost as if it were choreographed, he walked out and Grandma Fannie walked in.

When my parents' marriage was falling apart, Grandma Fannie began to visit more and more, and sometimes she took me to her apartment in Brooklyn. There I was made to feel special, like the world revolved around me, even if only for a few days. I helped around the house, and during the holidays, we baked some fabulous cakes and cookies. We sometimes walked around the neighborhood, met her friends, and even visited with many of my grandfather's family, whom she was still close to. Together, we'd sit and watch shows on the black-and-white television and then I'd sleep on the convertible couch, cooled by a small Westinghouse oscillating fan sitting on a wooden stool. Although temporary respites, these were simple, wonderful, and peaceful moments in my childhood.

Eventually, she moved closer to my mother in the Rockaways, where she lived until her death in 1982 after a long battle with diabetes. It was the first time I saw death in my family. In life, Grandma Fannie and my mother had remained close; they spoke every day, and she was my mother's best and maybe only true friend. But my mother was unable to get close to Grandma Fannie's burial site because it was not wheelchair accessible, so I said goodbye for both of us—goodbye to an angel who was there for me in some of my most difficult times.

Over the next few weeks and months, there was an increase in yelling, slamming doors, and more verbal abuse vomiting out of my father's mouth. It all happened at a frenetic pace until the point when my mother told me that a lawyer was coming to the apartment and to stay in my room. That was it—I was given no other explanation.

Finally, on the day that my father left the house carrying a suitcase, he asked me to go down to the garage with him. There, he told me he was leaving and that if anybody asked, for health insurance purposes, I should tell them that I live with him. That was it.

After he was gone, his entire family, including my grandparents, walked away from my brothers and me. Most of them I never saw again, and in more than four decades, I saw my father maybe five times.

My mother received very little money in the divorce, so we were left with barely enough to live on. At the time, the laws were not favorable to the homemaker, usually the wife, though the following few years saw tremendous change in financial equality and the laws between married couples. I think it's possible that my father was advised to resolve the divorce when he did or he would have to deal with a change in the law that would be unfavorable for him.

Finally, my mother's condition declined to the point that a home healthcare nurse (Lucille, whom I mentioned earlier) began coming in part-time to take care of her. She was a wonderful woman who ultimately took care of my mom for twenty-one years. But her job was to tend to my mother, not me. So that's when I began really having to take care of myself. No more Mom-cooked meals (though that stopped much earlier); it was up to me to make my own dinner or grab a slice of pizza, when I had enough money for food. Sometimes when I'd open the refrigerator door, there wasn't much there.

With a mother who was not well and getting progressively worse, I had to fend for myself. I had to determine what my essential needs were and how I was going to meet them. My goal was not to figure out what was a successful life but a successful day. I grew increasingly frustrated and resentful, and one day, I finally snapped. When I asked my mother for some money to get something to eat, she didn't have it to give—and I immediately reached out and slapped her. Sitting there in her wheelchair, she must have been stunned into silence, because she said nothing. But I knew right away I had done something horribly wrong. We never talked about the incident, but for years, I felt tremendous guilt, yet we continued to love each other as mother and son.

When I was in sixth grade, it was suggested that I be sent to a foster system in Brooklyn, a program for kids like me who had broken families. The people I lived with were very nice to me, but they were also very religious—the school I went to was a yeshiva, which was a Jewish Orthodox educational institution that focused heavily on Judaic learning. Since Sheldon was an Orthodox Jew and lived nearby, I stayed with him some weekends. But I never fit into that program. We never really practiced our faith at home, but my grandmother was more religious, and I think she thought the school would be good for me. Plus, it would give my mother a chance to figure out what she was going to do with her life and her health situation. Still, once I was there, one look around the room and I thought, "What am I doing here?" I knew right away I would never fit in.

After about a year and a half in the foster program, I was sent back to Far Rockaway to go to seventh grade in public school. But I struggled to actually make it to class. By the time I was in ninth grade, being absent from school became more of a pattern. Often, I walked around just observing what was going on in the world while everybody else was in school. I was never a bad kid, but I was certainly a lost kid.

WHAT I'VE LEARNED IN MY LIFE IS THAT STRONG RELATIONSHIPS MAKE US STRONG TOO.

When I turned thirteen, bar mitzvah age, my mother and grandmother scraped together enough and gave me a "party"—my mom, grandmother, and brother Cary were there, as were the ultra-Orthodox congregants of the synagogue where it was held. My father was nowhere in sight, didn't call, and didn't contribute to the event; about a year later, he sent me an empty card. After the service my mother had an "open house"—she left the door to the apartment ajar, and anyone who wanted to could come in for coffee and a slice of cake. A few of the kids I knew back then showed up.

When I returned to the public school system after being in the foster program, I had a few friends who I clicked with pretty well: Larry, who was a friend from an earlier time when we were both Cub Scouts; Mike, whom I had met in middle school; and Andy, who was a year older and who lived in the building next to me. Sure, there were a few other friends, but these guys were the regulars. While we all had plenty of laughs and while some may have had an idea that things weren't great for me at home, understandably, none of them knew the extent of the challenges that I was facing. Since I am friendly with them today, I'm sure they will be surprised to read about what they didn't know. Of course, how would they know anything beyond what most thirteen- and fourteen-year-olds know? How would I ever know as a young teenager how to begin to share my troubles with them?

When we initially come into this world, we are immediately introduced to our first relationships. For better or worse, it is our parents and siblings who nurture our ability to relate to other people. In my situation, especially in the early years, all those introductory people were inaccessible. Without having strong relationships, I went astray. I never felt like I fit in anywhere, even with the few friends that I had. They all seemed to have the perfect families—present fathers and healthy mothers.

All of us will get lost sometime in our life. We all face challenges of different kinds and at different times. And those challenges make us feel like we're completely and utterly alone. But we don't have to be alone.

What I've learned in my life is that strong relationships make us strong too. They help us grow our families, our businesses, and our lives. I've learned that anyone can build strong relationships—even a high school dropout with a sick mom and a deadbeat dad.

It took time before I found my way and eventually embraced all that life offered. And what I discovered was that the only way to be successful in life is to have real, authentic relationships. Whether it's in your personal or business life, strong relationships strengthen our core values and reinforce who we are. They allow us to reflect on where we came from and decide what part of our history we want to equip ourselves with—and what parts we want to leave behind.

THE ONLY WAY TO BE SUCCESSFUL IN LIFE IS TO HAVE REAL, AUTHENTIC RELATIONSHIPS.

In the next chapter, I'll share how, during my teenage years, I began to learn this powerful lesson—that going it alone just doesn't work and that building relationships is the best way to strengthen your life and empower you to overcome challenges.

ACTIONABLE SUCCESS MOVES

▷ Make a list of the top five people in your early life (childhood and teen years) who were part of the biggest and most influential moments (good and bad).

▷ Based on these people on your list, use three adjectives to describe each one. Use words that come naturally, and remember, this is not about positive or negative; it's about learning what has shaped your life at the beginning.

▷ Write down the three most memorable experiences from those early years.

▷ Looking at your background, name two family traits you would want to take with you through your life and two that you would abandon.

▷ Has anybody close to you been affected by an adverse health condition?

CHAPTER 2

FINDING YOUR PEOPLE
IT'S COOL TO BE YOU

Coming out of your comfort zone is tough in the beginning,
chaotic in the middle, and awesome in the end ... because
in the end, it shows you a whole new world.
—MANOJ ARORA

People familiar with me know that I'm someone who is sensitive on the inside but strong on the outside. Some people would even call me a mensch, a Yiddish word meaning someone who is genuine, who has integrity. That comes from being comfortable with yourself, being comfortable with who you are. As I told my son, Matthew, when he was dealing with some issues in middle school, "You're not a cool kid, so don't try to be cool. Stop pretending to be something you're not. Be the nice, sensitive kid that you are, and one day the world will think you're very cool."

It took me a while to learn that, but once I did, my life changed. That transformation came once I realized the power of being comfortable and genuine with other people—and with yourself. That allowed me to understand that what I thought was a weakness—being a sensitive kid—was actually a strength.

Admittedly, it was a rough start.

In 1976, when I entered Far Rockaway High School, there was a fairly large student population with its share of jocks, smart kids, cool kids, and nerds—all the typical groups you still see in any high school today. It was the prototype 1970s school like the ones you might have seen in a campy high school movie.

No matter the characteristics of the group, I just didn't seem to fit in. At the time, I still wasn't even sure who I was, but I believed that I had nothing in common with any of the different groups.

I really didn't know most of the other kids at school, so I wasn't aware of what their home life was like. But I imagined them going home from school, opening the door to a nicely decorated home, finding their mom waiting for them, grabbing a snack, and then waiting for their dad to come home for a nice family dinner. I imagined that each kid had a sibling who they got along with and maybe even had a dog.

It's not like I didn't know anyone in school; as I mentioned in chapter 1, I had a few friends who lived in the same development that I did. But they all had other friends who I never felt comfortable being around. Walking through the halls, no one shouted out, "Hey, Neal!" like they were happy to see me, so I just came to feel that the rest of the school population couldn't care less whether I showed up.

I was still dealing with the problems at home. So instead of thinking about school or making friends, I was always worried about adult stuff: my mother, her health, and money.

Although I made it through my freshman year, starting with my sophomore year, my absences increased—along with my intolerance for going to a place where I just felt isolated and uncomfortable, day in and day out.

In an effort to keep me in school, the guidance counselor proposed that I sign up for the "mini shop," which involved having would-be delinquents like me take three periods of a hands-on class and then have to attend only two academic classes. The trouble was that I felt no more comfortable being in shop with the muscle-bound auto-mechanic guys than I did being in classes with everyone else. In the first mini shop, I repaired typewriters that the students used in classes. When that shop didn't work out, they substituted it for the automotive shop. To this day, I'm no auto mechanic; I can't even believe I ever went under a car and did an oil change in that program. Unfortunately, while some of the kids in auto shop really loved it and actually went on to become engineers or mechanics, I still felt out of place.

So one morning, when I was sixteen, while everyone else was in class taking notes, or tests, or actually learning something, I walked into the administrative offices with a small handful of papers and the signatures required for me to drop out of school. I gave the papers to the large, gray-haired woman behind the counter who wore a pen as a pendant. She took off her glasses and looked at me with an expression that I interpreted as: "What a dumb kid. How could his parents let him do this?" Of course, on some level, I asked myself the same question. Unfortunately, I never got an answer.

I walked home alone, feeling a sense of relief. Dropping out didn't relieve me of my obligations at home, but I was no longer required to go to a place where I just felt uncomfortable all the time. I didn't have a grand plan or some unique strategy in mind, but I knew I had to get a job. I needed to make some money, buy food and clothes, and just try to survive on a daily basis.

Even back then, I was an early riser. Before I landed my first job, I'd get up and wander around and watch people. I saw what "older folks" did during the day, watched the delivery trucks pull up to the apartment complex, and even caught a few kids cutting school while I was legitimately out of school. Of course, I often walked along the boardwalk where I enjoyed the sound of the waves crashing or the smell of the ocean, both of which have always helped to momentarily clear my mind.

I ultimately secured several jobs over the next few years. From working in a fish store with my friend Mike to delivering newspapers to painting rooms at a nursing home with my friend Larry. At one point, I worked twelve- to fourteen-hour shifts as a busboy at a catering facility where I was paid $1.75 an hour. Not always fun, but it gave me some money to buy necessities.

Of course, I had other responsibilities besides working and looking for second jobs. My mother often needed a family representative at various governmental offices such as Social Security, Medicare, and Medicaid to ensure that her coverage continued. The job fell on me because my oldest brother remained in Brooklyn cloaked under the religious umbrella while Cary was always busy with his friends or girls. As I got older, I harbored resentment at my brothers for allowing me to do this solo. Though I was young and a dropout, I was able to clearly articulate to authorities my mother's very challenging situation. I often think that responsibility was the prelude to my becoming a lawyer because it was total advocacy on behalf of my mother.

One day, when I wasn't working and was out wandering around, I walked past the high school and was so relieved that I didn't have to go in. I didn't have to go there and deal with not being part of any real "group" of kids; I didn't have to feel that isolation in a crowd that always came with being in school.

It was at that point, when I was feeling utterly defeated and humiliated—a penniless high school dropout—that I took the first steps to changing the direction of my life.

As I walked away from the school, I passed a brick building that seemed familiar; paging through my mental index, I recalled going to preschool there, but then it was the Hartman Y. Originally built to serve the needs of a growing Jewish community, it had become a neighborhood center.

With nothing else on my schedule that day, my curiosity got the best of me, and I went inside to see what might be going on. I felt a sense of comfort as soon as I walked in. Maybe it was the familiar layout, or maybe it just brought me back to a time when my mother was able to still walk and life seemed a bit happier.

I was walking around and looking into the atrium in the center of the first floor when I felt a tap on my shoulder. "Can I help you?" I turned around and saw a young guy in his late twenties or early thirties with wavy, light-brown hair. Since there was no longer a reason for me to be in the building, I thought he was going to ask me to leave and maybe escort me out. Instead, he smiled big and introduced himself as Phil Goldberg, the teen director of the Y. "What's your name?" he asked. I told him and explained that I had gone to preschool in the building.

We started to talk, and he asked why I wasn't in school. It was an appropriate question, although I didn't have an equally appropriate answer. I could have told him I was cutting class, but that wasn't true. Or, since I looked older than sixteen, I could have told him I graduated and was looking for a job. Instead, I just said, "I'm not a school kind of guy."

He said, "Okay," without losing that smile and with no judgment.

Ultimately, that day was the first of what became an important and life-changing friendship in my world. Phil was the first adult outside of my family who I really felt comfortable with. Maybe because he was closer to my age than most adults I had really known up to that point, maybe because there were no lectures about dropping out, or maybe because he made me laugh with his jokes.

During the first year after dropping out, I visited Phil regularly. Sometimes he bought me lunch, and we would walk and talk and laugh—we laughed a lot. I helped around the center when he needed a hand setting up for a Jewish youth program for teens or some other youth group that was meeting for one reason or another.

I didn't know what a teen program or youth organization was, and I really didn't care to know. Since I had recently experienced living in a very religious environment—which didn't work out—I had little interest in joining any of the Jewish youth groups. I didn't think I had anything in common with them. But I had a friend, Melanie, who was president of the girls' chapter of one of those groups, B'nai B'rith Youth Organization, otherwise known as BBYO. Then and now, BBYO is a huge organization that provides a place for Jewish teens to get together for social and cultural activities.

A mutual friend had introduced me to Melanie the previous year, and she and I have been friends ever since. An honest and genuinely caring person, I saw Melanie as a trusted friend with a deep sense of integrity. She exuded intelligence with humor, which always made me feel comfortable, even though I was a high school dropout. Back then, I think she saw something in me that I didn't even see in myself. So while Phil was a good adult friend who I trusted and enjoyed spending time with, kind of like an older brother providing me guidance, Melanie was someone from my own age group whose opinion I came to value.

One day when I was helping Phil at the center, he said to me, "You know the girls' group meets here as well." As a sixteen-year-old having come from the Jewish all-boys school, I have to admit, that piqued my interest.

Melanie had also been telling me about her experiences with B'nai B'rith. For her, there were a lot of upsides and many benefits to belonging to—and leading—such a group. She told me there were parties and that it was a great way to meet people and, yes, there were plenty of girls to meet. "You'll have a good time," she said. "You'll do great."

At first, I still resisted. My religious exposure was pretty one-sided toward Orthodox Judaism—that was how my grandmother practiced, and it is where Sheldon navigated with my grandmother's help. So while I had tried to embrace orthodoxy, I leaned more toward the practices of my mother and my brother Cary, which were far from orthodox. But I came to find out that there was only a limited, strategic amount of religious exposure in the youth groups, and it was not Orthodox Judaism.

I also resisted because I just didn't want to try to fit in with kids who I thought probably came from "normal" families—kids who had a father and whose mother was not in a wheelchair. But I was curious, so I began asking Melanie more questions: "Do you think I should join?" "What are the girls like?" Finally, my curiosity got the best of me, and the endorsement by Melanie and encouragement by Phil convinced me to give it a try. For that I will be forever grateful.

Initially, I didn't tell any of my few guy friends—Mike, Larry, and Andy—that I would be going to a meeting for fear of being rejected by the only small group of kids that I was part of.

I got to the first meeting a bit early because the last thing I wanted was to be the new guy entering a room where everyone was already talking with their friends. I didn't want it to be like the first day of class in a new school when you walk in and try to find a seat. When I arrived, the room was set up with tables and chairs, but no one else was there yet. I began walking around and reading what was posted on the walls, pretending that I was interested in whatever I was reading—even if it was the alphabet that was plastered on the wall for the nursery school students who occupied the room during the day.

Soon the other members started strolling in, one by one. Some walked around, like I was doing, while others engaged in a bit of chitchat with each other. Nobody seemed too intimidating to me.

The next thing I knew, the then-president of the chapter, Mark, a cigarette-smoking guy with a gregarious personality, came over and shook my hand and we started talking. He introduced me to some people, and others came up and introduced themselves to me. The first meeting went well enough that I began going more regularly. Before I knew it, I found myself making friends with some of the others in the group. They just seemed like a group of friendly people who welcomed fresh faces. It became clear to me that the meetings were really social events where discussion was often about future social events.

After attending a few parties held with some of the girls' chapters, I really began feeling more comfortable with the group—and with myself. While I was hesitant to join the group because of its religious aspect, in truth, I think that commonality was one of the things that gave me some initial comfort. Although our religion was generally not the topic of conversation in any meeting—certainly none of the parties—it was a common background that we shared. No A-list or individual little cliques as were so rampant in high school. Just kids. Some were quiet, some were loud, and they came in all sizes. It was so nice to be in a nonjudgmental environment where I could just be me.

Before long, I felt so comfortable that I even thought my other friends might enjoy coming along and hanging out, especially those who were "half-Jewish"—in other words, one parent was Jewish and the other was not. I had a new group of friends and at the same time I brought in many of my friends from home, which added to the chapter's "fresh look" and led to many more social events. It was great because we had a building to hang out in and because there were other chapters that we could meet up with.

A few months after I became a devoted member—attending every meeting and all the parties as well as bringing in new members—the president, Mark, was stepping down. That left the position open: Who would be the next president?

It never crossed my mind that I might be up for consideration. I never thought of myself as outgoing or a leader and certainly not someone who could speak in front of a group. So when Mark approached me with the idea, I said, "No way. Find someone else."

But he was adamant. "It's easy," he said. So I tossed my hat in the ring, and as it turned out, my hat was the only one in the ring. Nobody else was crazy enough to want to be president, so I won.

I had mixed feelings about the idea, but I'll be honest: Although I was scared, I really did want to try it out. Sure, I was comfortable within the group, but being president would mean leading. No one had ever looked at me as a leader before. I guess I wasn't really a follower either—who did I have to follow? Still, I was a high school dropout, and now they were asking me to lead high schoolers?

I went to the guy with the smile, Phil, to get his advice. He was all in and said, "Of course you should. You'll do a great job, and I will help you." I couldn't recall the last adult who said that to me.

But before I agreed to do it, I asked Melanie what she thought, and she was also encouraging. She said it would be a great thing to do, and it wouldn't require as much of me as I thought it might. I weighed all the pros and cons, took a deep breath, and then told Mark, "Okay, I'll do it."

With that, I took my first few steps on what would become a journey of discovery about what it means to lead.

In the two years or so that I was involved in B'nai B'rith as chapter president, I gave multiple speeches and shook hands with hundreds of people, some of whom I still call friends. As it turned out, there was a lot more to being president of the chapter than going to parties and meeting girls. There were board meetings, regional and national conferences, and chapter integration efforts. Suddenly I was traveling. I was running meetings. I was delivering speeches. And most important of all, I was meeting people. I was building relationships. For the first time in my life, I had a community around me. And I wasn't just in the community; I was officially responsible for building and managing that community.

Since I had no formal instruction in public speaking, when I gave a speech, I just spoke as if I was having a casual conversation. Mostly I spoke to small groups, but a few of my speeches were to larger groups.

For me, there was always something cathartic about talking to lots of people; maybe it had something to do with the inability to talk to anybody at home.

> **THERE WAS SOMETHING AFFIRMATIONAL ABOUT PEOPLE MY OWN AGE COMING UP TO ME AFTER A SPEECH AND TELLING ME HOW MUCH THEY LIKED WHAT I SAID— EVEN MORE SO BECAUSE, WHEN I SPOKE, IT CAME FROM THE HEART.**

During my time as president, I found the social events to be truly awakening. The chapter was actually part of a much larger organization that included metropolitan, regional, and international leadership and conferences.

Maybe the most transformational part of being president was the positive input I received from my increasing number of friends who thought I was doing a great job. There was something affirmational about people my own age coming up to me after a speech and telling me how much they liked what I said—even more so because, when I spoke, it came from the heart.

It began to become more common for someone to shout, "Hey, Neal!" when I walked into a room. I really felt welcome; I felt like I had found "my people." And with that, I began to find myself. I was feeling good about who I was intellectually because I could speak to people, I could lead in a successful way, and on a personal level, people were actually drawn to me in some way. They enjoyed my company and wanted to be with me. With my involvement in the group, I became a little more open to sharing more about myself (although in baby steps). Was it me who changed? Did I wear nicer clothes? Was it my confidence that got a boost? Was it a combination of all of these?

The chapter also continued to grow in popularity, and I was proud that we were able to bring in dozens more new members. Of course, I met quite a few girls during my tenure in B'nai B'rith, and I would be lying if I said that didn't give me a significant boost of confidence. Prior to being part of this group, I had very negative feelings about what I looked like and how other people, especially girls, perceived me.

While I started dating a number of girls who I had met in B'nai B'rith, there was one who stood out. Gina lived in a town known as Belle Harbor, which was on the western end of the Rockaway Peninsula. Her neighborhood, unlike mine, was more upscale, with mostly private homes, many that were also near the beach. I met her at one of the B'nai B'rith parties.

I'm not sure what attracted her to me, but I know what attracted me to her: Besides being super cute and bright, she was very nice to me. She had a special way of holding my hand and looking into my eyes with her big blue ones. She told me how much she believed in my potential and how kind and sweet she thought I was. One time, leaning against a pillar in the basement of her house, where we spent hours hanging out and dancing, she looked at me and said, "There's just something about you, something different." She said it with a level of conviction that made me feel like she cared for me in a way that nobody had up to that point. She often visited me at the apartment and went out of her way to say hello to my mother. I didn't have a car, so I rode the bus to see her and always accompanied her on the bus back to her home. I always felt a little sad riding back home alone. But I remember with elation one of those visits: our very first kiss in the basement of her house.

Sadly, the relationship came to an end far too soon. Being so bright, she was aware that I was going through some major difficulties at home, and having recently dropped out of school, I was in need of some direction that she, at such a young age, could not offer me.

Several months later, my time with B'nai B'rith was winding down, and I was back on the dating scene. I guess I was just looking for a new connection or a bond. Raymond, a friend with whom I shared my first concert experience (Chicago), introduced me to a cute, short Italian girl who was about a year older than me and was not part of the B'nai B'rith group.

Jobwise, I had worked my way up to a position at Bloomingdale's. Turns out I was very good at selling men's clothes, so I ultimately moved into sales at the Calvin Klein counter. But even though I had a steady girl and a good job, there was still something missing.

Around that time, Phil suggested that I take my general equivalency diploma, or GED. The GED would allow me to get a diploma after passing a test that encompassed many of the core subjects most teenagers take in high school.

When I told the cute girl who I had met that I was thinking of taking the test, she jokingly replied, "You'll never do it." Now, I don't think she really meant to be callous. I mean, there I was, a dropout who was going from job to job (although I had a really good job at the time) and who had no real family structure. Yet there was something about her words that seemed to try to instill doubt. I thought to myself, "How could I have gone from one girl who thought so much of my potential to someone who thought I had so little potential that I would never even obtain a GED?"

I didn't blame her for doubting who I was and what I could do. But I felt I had made some real strides at B'nai B'rith. I not only had met some really great people but also had begun some sort of internal evolution. No longer did I assume that all I had was a few friends who didn't understand what I was going through. I had people like Phil, an adult who was trying to counsel me. I was able to do things that many of my friends were reluctant to do. I had a leadership role, spoke in public, met people all over the country, and became exposed to many people who either were going to college or were talking about going. I saw myself and the rest of the world on more of an even playing field—well, almost even.

In spite of the cute girl's doubts, or maybe because of them— maybe I took her words as a challenge—I began pursuing my GED.

The class that was given to help prepare for the GED test was at a local school much closer to where Gina lived. Beach Channel High School was new and, after almost two years of being a dropout, stepping back into the halls of a high school felt a little weird. Classes were at night, and many of the students were adults older than me who were looking to get their high school degree. Sometimes after getting off the bus, while walking toward the school in the dark, I wondered how odd it would be if I bumped into Gina. But I knew it was a slim chance: After all, why would she be there? She wasn't a dropout. But I wondered what she would say if she knew what I was doing. Would she be proud? And it dawned on me that trying to make someone else proud—especially a person who believed in me—was something that I had been doing most of my life.

I received in the mail the results that I had passed the test. When I opened the envelope, I was so happy, but other than that, there was no fanfare, no graduation party. But that was okay with me; I didn't want anything to basically signify some sort of stop because I now had some other plans to keep moving forward.

By that point, it had become clear to me: When I had no relationships, I had no prospects. But when I started to open myself and build a community of people around me, a community that included romantic relationships, the path to success began to lay out before me. Today I am a college graduate. I am a law school graduate. I am a loving parent. Much of that success is owed to the wonderful people with whom I've built strong relationships. Indeed, that's what I want for my children and for whoever else reads this book.

In this chapter, then, I hope you see what I mean by "finding your people." By creating and maintaining strong bonds with others, the types of relationships that are genuine and real, you can begin to find your own path to success.

BY CREATING AND MAINTAINING STRONG BONDS WITH OTHERS, THE TYPES OF RELATIONSHIPS THAT ARE GENUINE AND REAL, YOU CAN BEGIN TO FIND YOUR OWN PATH TO SUCCESS.

The next thing I learned on my own path

was how to acknowledge that we don't just want others in our lives, we need them—we need others in our lives in order to truly succeed.

In the end you don't so much find yourself as you find someone who knows who you are.
—ROBERT BREAULT

ACTIONABLE SUCCESS MOVES

▷ Name three things that you really enjoy doing that are separate and apart from your job or profession. No judgment, whether you like bird-watching, managing your kid's softball team, hot dog eating, or nude resorts—all that matters is that it is enjoyable to you.

▷ Name three things that you were afraid to do but did anyway.

▷ Name three things that you were afraid to do and never did.

▷ Describe the nature of the relationship and how you felt about relating to someone with a serious health condition.

CHAPTER 3

MOST GREAT MOMENTS INVOLVE OTHERS
ACKNOWLEDGING THE NEED FOR EACH OTHER

If you want to do really important things in life and big things in life, you can't do anything by yourself. And your best teams are your friends and your siblings.
—DEEPAK CHOPRA

If you think about it, the meaningful and worthwhile moments in life involve being with someone else. Whether it's friends, family, clients, or even just a temporary acquaintance, most of our greatest memories include someone else in the picture. Recognizing that is one of the first steps toward building powerful relationships.

Yet often we don't recognize the value of some relationships and just what a powerful impact they have on us until very late in the game. I learned that lesson through my brother, who started in life as my scourge, my tormentor.

Cary Goldstein always loomed larger than life, at least in my world. My earliest memories of my brother were of someone almost five years older who wanted to have nothing to do with me. After all, why would a fifteen-year-old want to spend time with a ten-year-old, even if it was his brother? In fact, he was more my own personal bully than a brother.

Let me share a few examples of what I mean. Remember that the apartments where we lived were in buildings clustered around shared terraces where people gathered: Kids played there, people sat on benches, and residents threw parties. In the warmer months, many kids would try to sell things to make a few dollars. They would get a wooden or cardboard box from the grocery store and then scour their bedroom for old comic books, Matchbox cars, or some other kid stuff to sell to someone else.

IF YOU THINK ABOUT IT, THE MEANINGFUL AND WORTHWHILE MOMENTS IN LIFE INVOLVE BEING WITH SOMEONE ELSE.

One day, I was playing on the terrace when I saw my brother with his friend selling their stuff, so I went over to see what he was getting rid of. Maybe I was being annoying or bothering him, but I don't recall that part; all I remember is him pushing me into the bushes and my ear getting caught in between some tree limbs; I began bleeding profusely from the injury. Of course, my mother couldn't take me to the hospital, so my friend's mother brought me to the emergency room, where I received several stitches to close the wound. I never knew whether Cary got into trouble for what happened, but that memory has stayed with me for fifty years. Not a good example of brotherly love.

In those early years, he was clearly "teaser in chief," saying and doing things that he knew would annoy me. Back then, it was not uncommon to hear my mother yelling, "Cary, leave him alone." In fact, up until high school, Cary was so mischievous that some would consider him a troublemaker. Most of his teachers at that time found him annoying, and he was far from what would be considered a model student. One time when he was in middle school, the police arrived at our front door to let my parents know that their son had stolen a bicycle, which really upset my mom.

When Cary was about seventeen and I was twelve, he had a steady girlfriend. One time, I followed them to see if I could catch them doing anything. I wasn't really sure what I was expecting to see, but he caught me following them and chased me away until I was far out of sight.

Just as I shared about myself in the last chapter, Cary also experienced an early evolution of his character, but his came with a distinct linchpin. In his final weeks of middle school, he was being so disruptive in class that a teacher told him that he would never amount to anything in his life. When he heard that, he took it as a challenge to prove the teacher wrong. From that moment on, Cary began a pivotal transformation. He changed his trajectory and became an A student in high school. I remember him studying at the kitchen table for hours on end, reading textbooks and writing away. When the yearly New York State high school regents examinations were coming up, he sat at the kitchen table and studied the red and white Barron's test prep review books for hours. His reward was a score of 100 on the tenth grade geometry regents test and a 98 on the eleventh grade trigonometry regents test.

In addition to improving his smarts, he transformed his personality—he went from being a troublemaker to being an outgoing and gregarious teenager who was truly liked by everyone. Just the mention of his name brought smiles all around. He was the epitome of the cool kid. He was smart, good looking, and nice to everyone. He didn't model himself after anyone—he was just his true self. During those times, even I wanted to be him—I no longer saw him as my tormenter.

When my father abandoned my brothers and me, Cary was about seventeen, and I remember him showing my mother how to use a checking account—Met Food Store: thirty-five dollars. Rent: one hundred fifty dollars. Seeing him sitting at the kitchen table and trying to help my mother with some of the adult responsibilities made him rise in my esteem—for a moment there, I even looked up to him.

Unfortunately, just as I was starting to battle my own preteen challenges, Cary was embracing independence. He already had a car by age seventeen, so he was often gone instead of being home and helping out with Mom. Even before he had a car, he was usually able to catch a ride with friends or even hitchhike to wherever he wanted to go—even to Florida on Spring Break. I'm guessing being gone all the time was his way of escaping the difficulties that handcuffed us both. For him it was by car while my only chance to escape back then came by foot or bus. Whatever the reason or mode, he was absent most of the time during my dropout years, and the majority of the care for our mother was left to me until Lucille, the home health caregiver, came in to assist my mother. His absence was something I resented for many years.

In time, however, my relationship with Cary evolved into one of the most positive ones of my life. Part of the evolution in our relationship involved a trip to the emergency room when I was in my teens. I had an argument with a girlfriend and was so angry that I ripped down the blinds in my bedroom. Unfortunately, those blinds were sharp and cut two of my fingers wide open. Immediately, I realized I had to go to the hospital, but again, I had no parent to drive me—by then my dad was gone, and of course my mother couldn't drive. Cary was in the other room, but at that point, I had never really asked him for help. Yet I had no choice. "Cary, Can you take me to the hospital?" I asked as blood spilled from my clasped hands onto the floor.

"Let's go," he said.

We crawled into his beat-up car that was missing part of the floor in the back seat. It reminded me of the cartoon character Fred Flintstone's car, where you just poked your feet through the floorboard to the ground and started running to get the car moving. Nonetheless, it was a car, and it was an offer of a ride. All the way to the hospital, I was very upset with myself and kept saying, "They are going to amputate my fingers—I just know it."

But in the calmest voice, Cary just said, "You're going to be fine." In typical Cary style, he even joked along the way and made us both laugh. Joking was a staple of his, especially in moments of difficulty. On that ride, I saw the beginnings of a new, and what ultimately became one of the most endearing, relationships in my life. Though I saw then the early steps in that direction, we were not there yet.

Several months after my visit to the emergency room, my doctor informed me that I needed surgery on my hand since it wasn't healing correctly. I had no insurance, so it was very upsetting when the doctor told me it would cost $500. Then I discovered that health insurance came with tuition at the community college I was attending (back then, that was more the norm). So, ultimately, I was able to work out the payment with the doctor for what wasn't covered by insurance, and we scheduled the surgery for a specific day, although it would require me to also stay overnight.

The surgery itself was successful, but the next morning as I was preparing to leave, the nurse came in and asked, "'Who's in the waiting room?"

I didn't have what I thought was the normal answer, like a mom or dad or other family member. All I could say was, "Nobody." Since it wasn't major surgery, and the walk home was only a few blocks, it was okay to discharge me from the hospital. The nurse brought a wheelchair to the room and pushed me to the front door. I thanked her and started walking home, a distance of only three blocks—but it felt more like twenty because I really began to think about the fact that there was no one waiting for me. It was a powerful reminder of just how alone I really was; it was a depressing thought but also a turning point.

On the walk home, I realized that, notwithstanding all the strides I had made up to that point, the building of relationships is a lifelong process. However you define your waiting room, you need people to be there. There simply is no wiggle room on that point.

HOWEVER YOU DEFINE YOUR WAITING ROOM, YOU NEED PEOPLE TO BE THERE.

I started to think that maybe Cary, my brother, was that person. But it would take more time and some real effort on both our parts for that to become a reality.

My lack of a car during that time in my life made it a challenge to get anywhere, including to Nassau Community College, where I was working toward an associate's degree. After I had received my GED, I was determined to further my education, and it was the best option for me. But without a car, it took three buses just to get there and back—a little over an hour each way. After the first semester, I was able to get my first car, a 1974 Dodge Dart. It cost $1,300, and all I had managed to save by then was $600; I needed another $700. So I went to visit my grandmother and told her the situation, to which she replied, "Go look in my top drawer and take what you need." I opened the drawer and underneath her grandma things—stockings and kerchiefs—was an envelope with a lot of cash. She never even asked me to pay her back; she was just like that.

Unfortunately, although I was able to buy the car, there came a point when I couldn't afford insurance for a few months. And while I'd never been stopped before, wouldn't you know it, during that window of time, I got a speeding ticket—without insurance, it was an automatic one-year license suspension.

Still, I fell in love with going to school, especially college. To this day, when the month of September rolls around, I always feel like going back to school—there's just something about the energy, the vibe, the idea of meeting people and creating new relationships.

After a few semesters of community college, I decided to pursue a bachelor's degree, so I went to Baruch College in New York City. It was quite a trek back and forth, so I only finished one semester before deciding the best solution was to go to school in Albany, a few hours from home. That would mean moving away to finish my degree. Although by that point my mother had Lucille, I still felt the need to be there. I was hoping Cary would help out with Mom in Far Rockaway so that I could go away to school, but I wasn't sure how to ask him. Finally, I asked for his opinion about the idea of pursuing my education away from home, and he said, "Go ahead. I'll be around for Mom." It was another step in our relationship—I was able to look to someone else to be there to fill a need.

I was scheduled to start classes at the University at Albany. Since I still didn't have a license, I wasn't sure how I was going to get there. Was I going to schlep my bags on the Greyhound bus? Was this going to be one of those "Who's in the waiting room for you" moments? Before I could even ask Cary, he offered to drive me. Wow! We had come a long way by that point.

The three-hour ride was filled with laughter. We talked about our family and the challenges we both faced in our own unique way, the kind of things that only siblings can understand. He also gave me advice: It was the first time I was going to live away from home (living in a foster home didn't count), and as someone who was very big on relationships, he gave me tips on how to make my way in the world and meet people (girls, in particular). Even though I'd already been through my tenure as leader of the B'nai B'rith and had developed some skills of my own in meeting people, it felt damn good to have a family member to talk to who didn't need my help or advocacy—it was really a first and like nothing I'd felt up to that point, and I soaked up every word.

My connection with Cary continued to solidify while I was in college. After a year and a half of going to school in Albany, I had to come home. I was living on student loans and the income from work-study jobs, which paid for many expenses but left little to live on. Ironically, one of my jobs was collecting donations for the alumni association, so while I was bringing in money for the school, my own money was depleting. I transferred to Queens College, which was much closer to home and much less expensive. It was also Cary's alma mater.

Coming home was interesting. Lucille was still taking care of my mom, so she didn't need me nearly as much. Most of my friends in Far Rockaway had moved forward with jobs, marriage, or relocating to somewhere else. My brother became one of my daily friends who I began to talk to regularly. He was navigating from a job in accounting into one in sales, the latter of which he seemed especially good at. While he had his own set of friends, he and I would often go out together when there was nothing else going on. We were each other's social safety net, and that was a 100 percent improvement.

Among our endless conversations were discussions about me going to law school. I had been contemplating it, but Cary always felt that was the road to success for me. Maybe it was because that was something he wanted to do (and would have been great at, in my opinion), or maybe he just felt that I had the right characteristics for being a good advocate. Ultimately I decided that law school was the right path for me, and with his wholehearted endorsement, I decided to apply.

I was not confident that I would be accepted to any law schools in the greater metropolitan New York area because they were extremely competitive. I felt that my dropping out of high school and having a GED and only a slightly better-than-average college grade point average were simply not enough. I could not afford to go to school full time during the day; I needed to work. So I applied to law schools with evening programs around the country in locations that most prospective law students were not running to. The New York schools were my "reaches."

When I began to doubt my decision, I asked Cary about going into law when there were so many lawyers already. At the time there were so many people applying to law school that I wondered how I was going to find a path to be successful. It didn't make sense for me to go to school for all that time, no matter where I went, if I was going to have difficulty finding a job or making enough money to pay back all the student loans. I remember Cary standing in the living room, looking at me as he fanned through the pages of a bulletin from one of the law schools, and asking, "How bad do you want it?" I don't really think he was looking for an answer because he kept on talking. "Who cares how many lawyers there are," he said. "If your clients like you, you'll do well." This was not some philosophical or existential theory he was relating to me. It was a simple statement of human behavior. People want to be surrounded by people they like, whether it's a personal situation or work related. Profound! I thought to myself, "I like people, and I'm pretty sure people like me." So I kept going with the process.

When the letters of decisions started to come, I was shocked. "We are pleased to inform you that you have been accepted." I was so happy but also felt a tremendous amount of humility. I couldn't believe I was being accepted to some of the most competitive schools in the metropolitan area. But Cary wasn't surprised—he had guided me in writing my personal statement simply by telling me, "Write about what you know—you. You already know how to speak from your heart; now write from your heart."

The personal statement was required by most law schools. It asked you to write about something that you felt influenced your desire to be a lawyer. What motivated you? It could be an experience, a challenge, or even another person in your life. Cary knew about personal statements because he had applied to law school before me; that was his initial career goal. During the application process, he was granted a rare in-person interview at one of the most competitive schools in the country, and during it, he told the committee his personal statement—about his family challenges and his own evolution in a very genuine and authentic way. He told me that there were tears in their eyes after the interview. He actually had been accepted into law school but instead ended up having a great career in textile sales.

Decisions to grant you entry into law school or other universities are made by human beings, so if you can authentically convey who you are, that is your best way to succeed. I could have painted any picture of my life to try to sound better just to get into law school, but I put all my cards on the table and prepared myself to go to whatever law school in the country that would take me. So when the decisions started coming in from the New York area, I was just blown away, and I think it was because of my personal statement. There's just something about digging inside yourself and figuring out what's driving you or who you are. That's your personal statement.

My brotherly relationship with Cary continued to evolve over the years. Sometimes we would get in the car and go for a drive just to spend time together. We'd ride along, making up funny stories about what we saw on the drive—who lived in this house, where that person worked, why the driver next to us made that choice of car. We talked about Mom and the progression of her illness. We talked about our grandmother and her great cooking or being at her apartment in Brooklyn. Our father, whom we hadn't seen in about ten years, was the subject of our ridicule. We talked about everyone but us.

Throughout our adult lives, our relationship continued to grow. Weddings, holidays, and even vacations with families were part of our sibling journey that I will always remember.

Life doesn't make any sense without interdependence. We need each other, and the sooner we learn that, the better for us all.
—ERIK ERIKSON

I'm so thankful that we were so much closer when, in January 2000, Lucille called and told me that, after a routine blood test, my mother had to go to the hospital because her white blood count was very high. In the emergency room, the doctor who had been examining my mother for what seemed like an eternity asked me if she had a do not resuscitate order, otherwise known as a DNR. I was bewildered. I knew it was an important document for families to make, especially for seriously ill people, but it came out of left field. My mother had been diagnosed with a fungating colorectal mass, meaning that it had been there for a while. The treatment would have been radiation and chemotherapy—tough treatment for anyone but excruciating for someone who was bedridden and confined to a wheelchair. At that moment, I knew she would never leave the hospital.

She remained lucid for a time and wanted to see her grandchildren who, at the time, consisted of my son, Matthew, and Cary's two daughters, Jessica and Shaina. She clearly knew the difficult situation she was in and at one point said to me, "I'm scared."

"So am I," I answered, "but we are all here for you."

Later that month, on a wintery cold Friday, I went to visit her, and she was disoriented. A CT scan revealed a blood clot in her lungs, and I was told to call all family members. When Cary arrived, our mother was on a morphine drip and drifting in and out of consciousness. When I saw Cary gripping the bed rails with his head down, I realized it was one of the few times I had truly seen his raw emotions. Unfortunately, it wouldn't be the last time.

About two o'clock that morning, I stepped out to get a cup of coffee at a nearby shop. The temperature was below freezing, but I didn't feel the cold, and while there were people and cars all near the entrance, I felt like I was the only person around. I reflected on my mother's life and her struggles and thought, "So this is how it ends." This was her reward for a life of pain? I wasn't angry, just resigned. My mother had lived her life, and in a short time, she would leave us.

Around seven the next morning, Cary stepped out for a few minutes, and shortly after that my mother's breathing became shallower. I whispered to her that I loved her and that she was the best thing that ever happened to my life, and I held her hand and wished her well on her new journey to be with her mom and dad. At one point, I turned my back to reach for something, and when I turned around, I realized she had stopped breathing. After she passed,

I removed her Star of David necklace that we had given her for her birthday. When Cary returned, I told him she was gone. He kissed our mother goodbye, and we walked downstairs. At that moment, I felt our bond was sealed because we truly shared something special that could never be replaced. I found that I really needed him at that moment, and for the first time, I realized he really needed me.

In the years that followed, Cary and I talked daily about anything and everything—except our relationship. I guess part of me was so happy that I had this amazing connection with my brother that I simply didn't want to rock the boat by digging deeper into any conversation about us. In fact, our relationship was much better than many of my friends had with their siblings. What a difference a few decades makes.

Soon after my mother passed, Cary and I started greeting each other with a kiss hello and a kiss goodbye. I can't say why we began doing it, but it further cemented what we had. He became not only my brother but also my friend and confidant.

After law school, it became about career paths and the development of clients. I decided that I wanted to truly give back to the community. Matthew, my son, was four and attending preschool at, of all places, the Jewish Community Center (JCC), a local chapter of the same organization that had been an integral part of my life early on. I had been approached to get involved with the center, and it didn't take long for me to say, "Of course." At first, I started a lawyers committee, which by all definitions was very successful. Within a year I was asked to sit on the board of directors for the JCC, which I was honored to do and would have remained in that position for as long as they wanted me. But they had other plans for me: They wanted me to serve as president of the organization. (When asked, my mind quickly flashed back to that moment when Mark asked me to be president of the B'nai B'rith chapter.) "I have to think about it for a few days," I told the committee. I needed time to figure out whether I was good enough to be the president of the organization. The old demons came crawling back, and I became preoccupied with what I believed were my own failings.

When I told Cary, he replied, "That's great!" in his robust voice, as if I had just announced a new family member was on the way. But he was proud, and you could tell by his tone.

"I don't know if I should do it. Do you think I should?" I asked, which was met with a few seconds of silence, as if he didn't expect that response. He clearly was not only proud of my achievements at that point but also, like the brother he became, he believed there was no end to what his little brother could do. He told me I was more than capable of doing the job, and I talked about how it could help my civic and business profile.

He then said something I will never forget: "Don't worry about that—it's good for the soul." He believed that you do what you truly have an authentic love for, feed your soul, and from there everything else will be satisfied. I accepted the position, and in my first speech to the community, I talked about how I had come full circle to help those in the community through an organization that had extended its hand to me. My time with the JCC as president was extremely rewarding, thanks in large part to a great team and the friendship and highly competent guidance of then executive director Arnie Preminger. Indeed for me it was the ultimate opportunity to give back to this organization that embraced me when I was younger.

After Cary's "soul" statement, I saw him as my go-to person because he knew how to guide and counsel me with sound advice sprinkled with enough spirituality to make it all seem just right.

One day in 2011, I received a call at work. It was Cary, who informed me that his blood tests showed abnormal enzyme levels in his liver and that he was going in for more testing. For the very first time in our relationship, I sensed a certain amount of concern in his voice. "I'm too young," he said. I knew he was heading to a dark place, but I replayed in my mind what he often told me during moments of difficulty: "You don't know anything yet, so there is no point in jumping to the worst place. It may be nothing, and if it is something, then we will deal with it." The news came back that his liver was diseased and would be controlled as long as possible with medication. It was way too early to consider a transplant.

Cary continued to work and enjoy family time, especially with his two daughters, Jessica and Shaina. I was in the wake of a divorce, so he and I were able to spend more time together. Holidays were fun and sometimes furious because of his passionate interest in politics.

Every year, he rented a beach house for a couple of weeks. In 2016, during his annual stay there, Cary had significant pain in his back and went to the hospital. He had a sepsis infection; with all the medication he was taking for his liver, his immune system was clearly compromised. He was in the hospital for a couple of weeks before being transferred to long-term care to help him rehabilitate his legs, which became somewhat immobile. We spoke at least once a day by phone, and since he lived in New Jersey and I lived in New York, I was able to see him once or twice a week.

The last time I spoke to him in person, we talked about the beach and how much he wanted to spend more time there. When I went to leave, I bent down to the bed to give him the usual kiss and hug, and I felt him hold me tighter. And then I felt his tears. The only other time I had seen my brother cry was at our mother's funeral. As he held onto me, he said, "You've been a great brother."

I replied, "I love you" and wouldn't let go until the tears subsided. As I left, I told him I would see him the following week.

He was released the next day and went back to the house he had rented by the shore. But a couple of days later, the pains started again, and he immediately went back to the hospital. On a Wednesday, I spoke to him by phone, and he was very talkative and said that his condition was stable. I had just purchased a new house at the beach, and I told him I was excited for him to see it. "I can't wait," he told me.

Then, on Friday morning, I received a call that he was in very serious condition and would probably not leave the hospital. I hung up the phone with shaking hands and a scattered mind. I picked up my niece, Jessica, who was working close to my home, and drove as quickly as I could to the hospital. By the time we arrived, Cary was heavily sedated and would never regain consciousness. I spent the next twelve hours or so with my nieces and the rest of the family, watching them make the difficult decision to remove life support. I hugged and kissed him, kissed his forehead, and told him to go be with our mom and grandmother, then I said my goodbye to my best friend, my financial guru, my counselor—my brother. It was a long and deeply sad ride home.

There will never be another Cary in my life. Ultimately, despite how tough the early years were, the loss of my brother would become one of the most devastating losses of my life. In a sense, his death made me feel more alone than I'd ever been—the man who had become my "waiting room" person was gone. His departure further revealed just how much I needed to continue to create powerful and genuine relationships if I wanted to lead a better life.

There is something truly unique about the family relationship. I'm not necessarily talking about blood relationships or that blood is thicker than water, as is often used to signify the alleged unbreakable relationship between family members. We all know that is not quite true for many people, my case in point. But I want everyone to find their "Cary," whether that's a brother or sister, cousin or friend. Find someone with whom you can have a truly inseparable bond. Someone who will give you counsel and advice no matter what time of day or night. Someone who will have your back even in the most difficult times.

Maybe that relationship hasn't appeared in your life or been accessible to you for one reason or another. Take a moment and look around at your family and friends to see if there isn't at least one person who you have a long history with but for whatever reason you never brought your relationship to its optimal point. For my brother and me, reconnecting was a matter of moving beyond our teenage antipathy and our determination to be independent. We had to acknowledge that we needed each other. That's essential in any relationship.

Often these relationships are bonded by longevity, but when that's not the case, look for those people who you can build that relationship with starting today. Each day that passes, your knowledge of each other's history will grow exponentially.

Remember: The real power of relationships is in those we build and nurture today, not just those we recognize in the rearview mirror for what they truly were. Few of the best, truly meaningful, most worthwhile things in life are done alone. Friends, family, clients—we need each other. We can't go it alone. And recognizing—and acknowledging that—is the first step toward beginning to build powerful relationships.

ACTIONABLE SUCCESS MOVES

▷ Write down three examples of moments when you needed other people to be there for you—in other words, your waiting room.

▷ Name three people who would be in your waiting room.

▷ Other than your spouse and children, name the last five people to whom you said, "I love you."

▷ Do you have a spiritual advisor?

▷ Do you feel you need other people? Why or why not?

CHAPTER 4

LISTEN MORE THAN YOU TALK
LISTENING IS GIVING

*Listening is such a simple act. It requires us to be present,
and that takes practice, but we don't have to do anything
else. We don't have to advise, or coach, or sound wise.
We just have to be willing to sit there and listen.*
—MARGARET WHEATLEY

As I discovered with my brother Cary, sometimes relationships take
time to really gel. As family, there was a bond that brought us together
after our youth that allowed us to build one of the strongest relationships of our lives. But in some relationships—for instance, those that
are legally bound in some way—it can be more difficult to find a
common bond when things don't quite seem to be working out.

Marriages, for example, can be very difficult relationships to
maintain; in some marriages, of course, children tend to keep parents

together. But when communication—or lack thereof—is a major issue, sometimes staying together is a worse choice than calling it quits. Still, I found that even an acrimonious marriage that ends in divorce can ultimately turn into a very meaningful friendship that benefits everyone. All it takes is learning to listen more than you talk. I found that out in a marriage that ended after twenty-five years but then became a trusted friendship.

It ended with the two of us in separate conference rooms. Mine was a huge space with over a dozen chairs surrounding a gaudy table where only my lawyer and I sat, and he handed me a fifty-page document—the final divorce agreement. As I sat there reading through it one last time, wanting to make sure everything was spelled out just right, a sense of loneliness—and relief—overwhelmed me for a moment. Yes, I have been a lawyer for many years and have seen clients in similar positions, but I had never been the one to feel that sense of solitude when recognizing the gravity of the moment. Divorce inevitably is about two sides of an equation, and by signing on the bottom line, I knew my life was going to dramatically change. I knew I would be seeing less of my children, who were crazy about me and I was crazy about them, and that I was walking away from a relationship that had been a part of my life for two decades. With that, I signed in all the areas where my name was printed alongside the name Vicki Goldstein.

I met Vicki in Long Beach in 1983. I was attending my sophomore year of college in Albany, going to classes during the day, and working retail at night, whenever possible. On the weekends when I had time, which wasn't often, I would go home to Far Rockaway and go out with some friends. My social life at the time was limited, so one weekend when my friend Mike said, "C'mon, let's go out. You'll have some fun," I quickly agreed.

We drove over the Atlantic Beach bridge separating Far Rockaway from Long Beach and headed to a bar that I had not been to before, ordered drinks, and scoped out the crowd, especially the girls. I hadn't had any real relationships for a while, so on the one hand, I was ready to meet someone, and on the other hand, not so much. Part of me even felt like giving up on any romantic relationships because nothing had been clicking for me for at least a year.

We started talking to a group of three girls, all of whom were cute, but I was clearly more interested in talking with one of them in particular. She was on the shorter side (which I preferred because I was no giant), a brunette (which I also preferred), and had a great smile. Her name was Vicki, and she worked at a major upscale department store in the city.

After having a few drinks, Mike and I walked with the girls over to the beach, which was only a few minutes away. At some point after rolling around in the sand a bit, Vicki realized she had lost her car keys. It was nearly 2:00 a.m. and she needed to get home and drop off her friend as well. Vicki tried calling another friend who she thought had an extra key, but that didn't work. So what was left to do? Call her parents. I asked her, "Are you kidding me? This is how I have to meet your dad?" I was thinking, "This guy is going to go nuts on me." But I certainly would never leave her alone at that time of the morning.

About a half hour later, a red pickup truck drove up, and the driver rolled the window down, but before he could say anything, Vicki asked, "Is Mommy mad?" Her father just smiled. That was it. That was the beginning.

Vicki and I dated for the next year or so, and I met her dad, Mike (the guy with the smile in the pickup truck); her mom, Marie; and her brother, Frank. Her family was very nice and always very hospitable.

I was invited to a few Sunday dinners and, wow, if you never had a true Italian Sunday dinner, you're missing out. Appetizers, wine, great bread, sausage, more bread, sauce, and more bread. Always some desserts. I thought it was fabulous.

One fall, Vicki and I took the railroad into Penn Station; she was on her way to work, and I was heading back up to Albany. She was saying goodbye and asked, "Are you okay with money?" Of course I told her I was fine, but I wasn't and never had enough. Anything I earned was spent on food, clothing, and what I needed to live on my own in Albany. But she sensed my need and quickly reached into her pocketbook and dug out twenty dollars for me. Up to that point, I had very rarely asked for money from my mother since she had very little, let alone what may be her last few bucks. But that was Vicki. She was a generous and giving person, which I had rarely seen up to that point.

In 1985, after almost two years of dating and at the ripe old age of twenty-three and twenty-two, we decided to get married. I had known from a very young age that I wanted to get married and have children. When most kids were thinking about prom, I was thinking about creating a family. At the time, I believed this was the moment for that to happen. I thought marriage meant that we would have a happy home, and I would have people around me who acted as a family unit, but then what does a twenty-three-year-old know about the factors to be considered when getting married? In hindsight, I sometimes even wonder if those Italian dinners entered into my decision to get married. But I always wanted to have children too. For me, there was never a second thought about that. I wanted to be able to break the cycle of fear and anger, disappointment, and frustration that I had experienced in my own upbringing, and marriage represented that first step.

Many friends were getting married at the same age, in their early twenties, unlike today when more people are waiting until their late twenties or even longer. Back then, nobody tapped my shoulder and asked, "Do you want to think about this?" or "Are you sure? You're pretty young." Quite honestly I wasn't looking for a second opinion; I thought this was what you were supposed to do. This was part of the journey. Meet a nice girl, fall in love, get married, and have children.

In truth, today I would discourage my own children to marry at that early age. I'm not saying it couldn't work, but the mature adult brain really isn't completely formed at that point. In our early twenties, we just haven't lived long enough to make some of the best judgments about things. But I was in law school and feeling pretty good about myself and thought marriage was the next step on that path to success.

The early years of our marriage were fairly straightforward. We both worked during the day. I had found a job as a law clerk for an extremely busy personal injury practice and attended law school at night. Once an opening became available in the law office where I was working, and with my encouragement, Vicki started her legal career and ultimately worked as a paralegal for a very high-end law firm in the city. We both had a strong work ethic and enjoyed our respective jobs.

On the weekends we did what other young couples did: we hung out with friends and often went to my in-laws' house for that delicious Sunday dinner, which usually started in the afternoon.

But, in hindsight, I realize we didn't spend a lot of time talking with each other. That may seem like an odd observation to make, but it probably was a fairly significant factor. Without talking there is simply not much connecting. Having grown up in a family where there was a complete lack of communication, you'd think I would have known better. We weren't talking like a young couple should; we weren't getting to know ourselves and each other. We weren't growing together.

In truth, I'm not sure when I started noticing issues within the marriage. After several years I certainly noticed a change in Vicki's attitude toward me. At the time, I chalked it up to different response mechanisms from different human beings. I'd ask her what was wrong and she would just reply, "Nothing" or "It's not you; it's me." But I tried not to press her further because I didn't want to rock the boat. After all, I had finished law school and had a good job, a nice apartment, and a family that embraced me.

But the marriage began to ebb and flow, with moments to the extreme one way or the other. As I shared earlier, Vicki was an extremely generous person. She was the first to help a friend, share a recommendation, buy a gift, invite somebody over for dinner, and assist someone in need. But somewhere along the way, she began to have very intense, and very emotional, mood swings. Sometimes she would act as though she felt slighted at alleged offenses that were, to others, minor or even nonexistent. Toward me, she was becoming very controlling, often answering questions that were directed at me and taking charge of conversations to the point that I found it difficult to talk. At times, she might ask for my opinion about something, but when I gave my answer, she would get irrationally upset that I hadn't given the response she wanted to hear. The few times that I tried to have a reasonable discussion with her or ask her what was going on, I was met with silence or with yelling and accusations that I was imagining everything.

Most people do not listen with the intent to
understand; they listen with the intent to reply.
—STEPHEN COVEY

Over time, communication, in all forms, became shallower and ultimately broke down completely. As much as I wanted to have children, I delayed the discussion because I simply wasn't sure that the marriage was viable. Since we never really had the "children discussion," I didn't know if there was also reluctance on her part. Maybe she was thinking the same as me. What was clear is that, although we both really wanted children, we were avoiding the actual decision to pull the trigger.

Then, in 1996, eleven years after we were married, we had our first child, Matthew. I think at that point the strong desire to have a child and simply accepting that there are pros and cons to any relationship led us both to the decision. I loved my son so much that after he was born, to keep peace in the family, I simply stuck my head back in the sand.

In 2002, we had our second child, Sari. The marriage was still difficult, but we wanted Matthew to have a sibling who he could share his life with. I know that only children are well adjusted and have very successful relationships with friends and family. However, I was hoping for Matthew to have a sibling with whom he could have the same experience that I had with my brother Cary. That's something that's irreplaceable.

Sari came into this world with plenty of tumult. Vicki had an amniotic embolism during childbirth, and she almost died. It's a condition that only occurs during childbirth and often has devastating results. When it happened, I was whisked out of the delivery room, and forty-five minutes later, after hearing "code blue" and watching an army of doctors rush into the delivery room, the waiting room door swung open. The doctor entered and brought me our baby wrapped in blankets and said, "Your wife is not going to die. We controlled the bleeding." He handed me Sari, and I looked at our little miracle.

I was allowed to go back into the delivery room where everything was cleaned up; you wouldn't know tragedy had been narrowly averted. I leaned over Vicki, who was sedated, and told her the baby was okay and that I would stay at the hospital. I stayed in the room until she fell asleep.

After Sari was born, I think the trauma was permanent for Vicki. To compound the feelings I'm sure she was battling after having nearly lost her life in childbirth, five years later, she developed a tumor and lost her vision in her left eye. Often depressed and despondent, her relationships with friends and family worsened.

In 2011, after years of progressive fighting and attempts at trying to make the relationship meaningful, I made the decision that it was in everyone's interest to separate. It is not easy after twenty-five years to break a relationship, let alone a marriage. My primary concern was the physical and mental well-being of my children, and that, in fact, was the impetus for the decision.

Although I believed that the separation and subsequent divorce were in the best interests of my children, ultimately, they were in everyone's best interests. For me, it was a nightmare being relegated to seeing my children only a couple of times a week and having to engage in conversations tinged with accusations and insults that came with the divorce. It was very difficult for the kids, who were in the crosscurrents. Yet I believed we were and are the better for it. My conversations with Vicki, when not tinged with anger, were terse and were much more like the negotiations I have as a lawyer with my adversaries. In fact, the matrimonial legal system is like running on a hamster wheel; you could run forever and still wind up in the same place. I now know why it was not an area of practice I wanted to get into.

Finally, that cold winter day at the end of 2012 when we signed the divorce decree and walked out of the lawyers' office, we said our goodbyes.

Little did I know then that our relationship was in the midst of an evolution that would take us to a completely different place.

Over the next several years, Vicki and I found ourselves talking more and arguing less. Indeed, I'm not sure I remember any arguing at all. Was it the time? Was it the lawyers? Was it that we just needed to move on? Was it doing the best we could for the kids? I really don't know, but I can definitely say it was easier communicating with Vicki when the anger ceased and we were able to talk—and listen.

Of course there were always continuing conversations about the kids and schools and behavior, but there were also many times when she would simply say, "Neal, can you give me advice?" She often asked me about things she never would have talked about during our marriage. "Neal, I'm selling the house and buying a townhouse—should I pay cash or finance it?" I felt that she really valued my opinion at that time, something I did not feel early on, so I really wanted to give her the best advice that I could. She was truly reaching out for friendship, and I extended my hand.

During those years, in the wake of the divorce, we were not just hearing what each other said, but we were actually listening. Anyone can hear what the next person says, but listening is a quality many people think they have but few actually do. In any marriage or partnership, all it takes is one person who is more interested in being heard (namely, talking) and less interested in listening, and the relationship is doomed to fail. What Vicki and I had after the divorce was real communication.

LISTENING IS A QUALITY MANY PEOPLE THINK THEY HAVE BUT FEW ACTUALLY DO.

As a result, we were both able to share in the kids' graduations and birthdays without any feeling of discomfort. Even after I remarried in 2016, my relationship with Vicki continued to evolve—and in a way you might not expect. A friendship grew between my wife and my ex-wife. Vicki became an integral part of the holidays, and with my stepdaughters, Jessica and Lana, also present, the relationship seemed truly comfortable. Everyone got along, and it felt great to have family celebrations with so much harmony.

At the close of 2017, during the holidays, the boundaries of our friendship were truly tested. My wife and I were invited to Vicki's place for dinner on Christmas Eve. We had already been to each other's homes for dinner and some holiday celebrations that season. In keeping with Vicki's gregarious and outgoing personality, there was fun and laughter and all was good. But Vicki had complained during the evening of a headache and was just not feeling herself.

Within the following week, Vicki went to her doctor, and after some initial visits and referrals, a recommendation was made for a CT scan to see if there was something more going on than just a simple headache. Vicki called me with the test results: the doctor suspected a tumor. Her words quickly took me back to when my brother had called to tell me that his liver tests came back abnormal. Of course, like my brother, I said, "Let's not go to the worst place. We don't know for sure just yet, and even if there is something, treatments are generally available." We would come to find out that "generally" was the operative word in my statement.

After the diagnostic exams, Vicki's first appointment with her oncologist would be, by most standards, a nerve-racking experience. Most physicians want you to bring someone with you to the appointment, someone who you have a strong relationship with and who will listen carefully, no matter how difficult things may get during the office visit. Of course, you want someone who you can share your emotions with if that moment should arise. Vicki picked two people to go with her. A long-time friend, Susan, who had stood by her side for the past twenty years, and my wife, whom she had known for only a few years. I was surprised and humbled that she wanted my wife next to her. It was a significant sign of just how far our relationship had evolved after the divorce, from cordially dropping off the kids to inviting each other in for a cup of coffee, then dinner, then the holidays, and now a shoulder to lean on in a time of need.

I waited for news of the appointment. My mobile phone rang, and it was my wife. I knew I was going to hear some news but nothing like what came. "She has stage four lung cancer that has metastasized to the brain." I was standing in the lobby of my office, and everyone knew by my reaction that the news wasn't good. My mind was all over the place. Yes, I was thinking of our children, but I was also thinking of Vicki and what she must be going through.

Over the next six weeks, Vicki had some periods of, some would say, better moments and what seemed like many tough ones. When I first visited her in the hospital, it was difficult to see this woman whom I shared a life with for so many years, so we kept the conversation light. When she came home, we were all there for her. On one of her radiation visits, she asked if I would take her, and without hesitation I said yes. It was a tough day for her because she went to the hospital first to have a port inserted for upcoming chemotherapy and then after that had her radiation treatment. In between we went out for lunch, and we sat and talked about the kids. I really wanted to just listen to anything she had to say and wanted her to feel that she had the moment and could say anything. Surprisingly, Vicki did not bring up anything about her prognosis, or any past history of ours, which was her prerogative. She just wanted to have lunch like a regular person, and that's exactly what we did.

During the last month of her life, I received some very nice text messages from Vicki. After sending her a recent picture of our daughter, Sari, and me, she sent me the following text: "She is one lucky girl to have you! Thank you for always being there for her. You're a great dad." A few days earlier, I had sent her a recent video that I had shot for my law firm, and I quickly got this message: "You wouldn't be who you are without your mom. Truly an amazing woman. You are just like her." Another text she wrote: "So proud of you. You truly are a very special father, son, and husband."

When I last saw Vicki, she had difficulty sitting up. I told her that her dad was watching over her, and she replied, "I know." I told her that the kids would be fine, and she replied, "I know they are in good hands."

I kissed her on the forehead and said, "Get some rest." But we both knew.

Two days later, Vicki's mom called to tell me she had passed.

What is it about the relationship of a marriage or life partnership that makes it so special? Why are so many spouses and partners not talking to each other or expressing their true feelings? Why are so many of us involved in some of the most cherished relationships of our lifetimes not in sync? Why are we not listening to each other?

When we look for that "special person," do we really look for some special and unique person who jibes with our values? Probably not as often as we should, especially if we haven't truly identified what our values are. It's not simply that "I think stealing is wrong and so does she so we're good." Are we rowing in the same financial, health, educational, and spiritual direction? That's not to say we can't have some differences in our political choices or our movie genre preferences, but do we stand together in how we look at the greater avenues of life?

Often, especially when you're younger, it's harder simply because you don't know where you yourself stand. What's important is that we continuously check in with ourselves even at an early age to see where we stand and if that special person is the lifetime partner who makes sense. It's not easy, but it's a must if you're looking to avoid the challenges that will inevitably arise when life comes knocking at the door—and it will.

When we're young, we're more about physical chemistry and having a good time, and there is nothing wrong with that. But if you've left all the other value checkpoints to the side, then prepare for the following: Knock, knock. Who's there? Life, and you must answer the door together. Will you both be ready?

LISTENING MAY BE THE MOST IMPORTANT FACTOR IN DETERMINING HOW AUTHENTIC YOUR RELATIONSHIP WILL BE.

When allowing another person into your life, whether a spouse, a partner, or a friend, you must be prepared to listen. Listening may be the most important factor in determining how authentic your relationship will be. When you are truly listening to someone in your life, you can't be talking, period.

Though this story started out as a marriage that didn't work, it morphed into a friendship that did. I've been blessed in my life with many people who I consider to be friends. Sure, some are closer than others, but authentic and genuine friends truly listen when you are talking. Conversely, they allow you the opportunity to use your unique human listening skills for their benefit.

Listening, indeed, is giving. You are giving yourself to another so that, for the time that they are talking, you are in the moment. If the person is truly your partner in life or your authentic friend, then you will be all ears. You must listen with your ears—and your eyes. The true listener has their eyes fixated on the other person because nothing does more for listening than looking at the person who is talking.

Most of the successful people I've known are the
ones who do more listening than talking.
—BERNARD M. BARUCH

The "real" listener listens with reflection, compassion, and sympathy and should be able to regurgitate what the other person is saying with the same emphasis on feelings, concerns, anxiety, happiness, and sadness. In fact, your listening skills have to include your heart and soul. With your heart you must have empathy skills ready. Listening with your soul means listening so that your inner instinct, wisdom, and voice are aware of what is being talked about. It's really what we use to give guidance, counsel, and insight if asked by the speaker.

Without the skills of listening, true authentic relationships can never exist.

ACTIONABLE SUCCESS MOVES

▷ Write down the names of three people with whom you have lost contact but would like to renew your relationship. With each person, send a text or an email or give them a call to simply say, "Hi, I've been thinking about you." Then write down how that makes you feel. There is no guarantee of a successful outcome, but more than likely you will have reignited a connection that you've wanted for some time. Indeed, you wouldn't have written that name down unless that person was somewhere in your mind. This is an exercise that will help you gain control over your relationships.

▷ In your current relationships, do you listen to your partner? Try this: Have your partner talk to you for three minutes about something on their mind. The three minutes are theirs. Listen to what they have to say. When the time is up, repeat what you believe you heard. Ask your partner if they feel that you listened carefully. Then trade places.

▷ Are your relationships flexible? If not, name two things you can do to try to solidify them.

▷ Have you renewed any relationships from the past? Is it different now? How?

Mom at the left was quite popular and had lots of friends when she was young.

Mom loved her early years when she traveled and dressed impeccably (maybe late teens or early twenties).

Mom had a love affair with the camera.

This was the "terrace" where all the action happened. Apt. 1A was right behind my "vehicle."

Never thought I was chubby but this picture tells a different story. On the terrace when one of the older folks gave me his seat and radio.

Honestly I don't remember this picture, but it's the only one I have of me holding my mom's hand, so I treasure it.

At that age I always wanted to be in the background. The walker for me sent the message, "Your mom's different." Cary with Mom.

PS 215 Elementary School picture—I hated ties with plastic clips.

Somewhere in between cool and me.

Cary's HS picture and his "lion hair."

Melanie was and always will be a great friend. Her advice early on was key to so much positive change.

I tried being all kinds of cool most of the time. It simply wasn't me.

Mike and I hanging out on the roof of our apartment building. He knew I had issues at home, but how much did he really know?

1978 and sixteen: Things are starting to change. I was never the cool kid until I didn't give a shit, then I became cool.

From left: Mike, me, Andy, and Larry hanging out at someone's house.

Where I lived the beach was the place to be. Here on a fall day sitting on the jetties and with the help of her jacket and photography skills, Dana Feinberg, a friend, snapped the shot.

Larry and I met in the Cub Scouts, and here I am the day before his wedding. We still talk regularly.

Law school graduation yearbook. Well, it was four years of sweat, stress, and success.

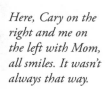

Here, Cary on the right and me on the left with Mom, all smiles. It wasn't always that way.

From left: Mike, Andy, and myself, still friends.

*Sharing your story is one of the golden keys to creating
authentic relationships.*

This is how I will always remember Cary, all smiles.

Here with Gina at one of our favorite areas, the central coast of California. Making the ordinary extraordinary.

CHAPTER 5

FACE-TO-FACE CONTACT
MAKING THE ORDINARY EXTRAORDINARY

*Joy comes to us in moments—ordinary moments. We risk missing
out on joy when we get too busy chasing down the extraordinary.*
—BRENÉ BROWN

It's a cool, crisp autumn day. A divorcée in her forties is sitting in her
kitchen with a cup of coffee and checking her Facebook messages
when she notices one from a mostly bald man claiming to be Neal
Goldstein. Not recognizing the image, she opens up his profile and
takes a closer look at his picture. He might have a lot less hair, but
it's Neal all right. The same Neal Goldstein she dated when she was
sixteen. The same guy whose potential she had believed in so much
back then but who was so lost that he could have gone in a completely
different direction. Then she starts digging. Then she starts crying—
crying because she discovers that he did make something of himself.

The teen who had dropped out of school and had so many challenges at home was now a successful lawyer; he had managed to overcome the adversity of his youth. She recalls the struggles that he was having with his mom and how difficult it was and then she messages back: "Of course I remember you."

That was the start of how I reconnected with Gina and how I would soon discover that there can be something truly extraordinary about very ordinary moments.

At first, Gina and I just communicated by phone and text, but over time, that wasn't enough, and we finally met again face-to-face.

That's how to build genuine relationships that can help you become more successful in your personal and professional life. When it comes to cultivating relationships, it takes more than just connecting via social media, text, or email. It takes getting together face-to-face.

Face-to-face is the only way we're able to touch others—to shake hands, pat someone on the back, put your arm around them, or give them a hug. It's the only way to truly listen to what they're saying in a real sense.

Sure, a company website can inform potential clients and bring in new business, but that online presence only goes so far. In my own business, it's when the client actually meets me in a conference room, or better yet, at their home or a coffee shop, that the relationship becomes more feasible. That face-to-face contact is the only way the client really gets to know who I am, really gets to see my nonverbal cues and begins to understand how genuine I truly am. Maybe it's looking directly at the other person, the placement of your hands, or even how you enter a room that simply can't be measured by digital means and that sends signals of trust.

Social media and online technology are great ways to initiate a relationship, but they are not the best for deepening one. I found that out after my divorce.

Having gone through a tumultuous separation and divorce, you never really know when you're ready to open yourself up to another person. Eventually there comes a moment when you realize that you need to rebuild or create new, soulful relationships that are even deeper than the genuine and authentic relationships that I talk about. There comes a point when two people connect in a way that is extraordinary. When we find someone with whom we are willing to share the journey of life, then we can begin to experience what it means to reach the true, best version of ourselves.

After the separation, there came a point when I felt that I was running on empty and really needed to rebuild. Although I had built my life and moderate success on genuine and meaningful relationships with others, and I had social media friends and others, like my brother, to turn to, I still felt an emptiness. I felt like I needed something more. Most of my connections were distant in some way— either by physical distance, as was the case with my brother, who was also busy with his own life, or, as I mentioned, by being in an online environment or being a professional connection.

So I began to search for old friends who maybe wanted to reconnect and thought I might even make some new friends along the way.

I knew that relationship-building is a lifelong process that occurs over time as our place in the world changes. Maybe it's a new job, a death, a health issue, or a divorce. Or maybe it's someone from our school days. That led me to think of Gina. I remembered how she always had kind words for me and how she always seemed to look at me with those blue eyes as if she had great confidence in me and my abilities.

Even though we had gone our separate ways because we were so young and I had so much going on, I really wanted to reconnect, in part just to let her know that I was okay after all—I had done pretty well for myself and had accomplished so much, in spite of her concerns. I have since seen that same sentiment in many people who I've reconnected with—they're surprised to find out that I went from high school dropout to lawyer. I'm not going to lie: it feels damn good to let people know that you beat the odds or that the underdog won.

Reaching out to Gina was pretty straightforward. Her last name then was not common, so I thought it would be easy to locate her. Facebook had gone from being a platform for younger people to one that was primarily a way for baby boomers to reconnect, so I took a chance, and sure enough, I found her and messaged her.

That message led to a phone call, and when I heard her voice again after so many years, she sounded like the same teenager I remembered. Same voice, same laugh—the ability to laugh has always been important to me (but not the most important feature that I find attractive—which is not what you're thinking! More on that later). In our first call, we talked and talked—for three hours. Yet when I hung up, I really had no thoughts other than maybe I was rebuilding a friendship with another person who was single. Still, I really wanted to meet her face-to-face. I wanted to see what she looked like after all those years, and I simply wanted to hear that laugh again in person.

We agreed to meet up at an informal reunion of some friends whom we both knew when we were younger. When I arrived at the event, naturally I was nervous. Having been in the married-guy phase for so many years, it was at first an uncomfortable experience being single at a gathering. Would I say the wrong things? But there were other single people there, as well as couples, and I knew some of the people in attendance. Plus, it wasn't like I was going to meet Gina with any specific intent in mind; I really was hoping to rekindle a friendship. Ultimately, I knew if I was just myself, people would embrace me for who I was. I've always found that being your authentic self is the way to win people over, and I've tried to be that way with everyone I meet. Whether it's a judge in a courtroom or the sanitation worker who empties my trash container, I try to relate to everyone.

So I decided to be myself, the genuine and authentic me, and to connect with others as I knew how to do, in the hope that I would form some new relationships.

I arrived to a crowded room with music from the 1970s playing. I looked around and didn't see Gina, but I was certain I would recognize those blue eyes when she walked into the room. Then in came a woman still wearing sunglasses, who walked with such a sense of unpretentious confidence that I knew right away it was her. After about six seconds of embracing a few friends, she made a beeline straight to me. To this day I'm not sure how she recognized me so quickly, but I was so caught off guard that I didn't know how to think or react. Sure, I'd had days to prepare, but it simply wasn't enough.

I quickly gave her the old-friend hug followed by: "Hi. How are you? You look great. So we finally get to meet after our telephone conversations." In truth, I'm really not sure who said what, but we talked about everything from school to grandparents and everything in between. Gina really seemed interested in how I was able to change the direction of my life since we last saw each other. She later told me she was so happy to see how I had turned my life around and was quite frankly surprised at herself that she wanted to know so many details about how I did it. We also laughed and laughed and laughed some more.

I began to feel this could certainly be a nice friendship but maybe also something more. During that three-hour, in-person meetup, I saw her eyes connect with mine in a way that I had long forgotten. We had spent hours on the phone before that meetup, but that face-to-face connection made me feel that our friendship truly was so much deeper.

When it was time to leave, I walked her to her little two-door car and said, "It was great seeing you, and I hope we can see each other again." With my hand on her shoulder, I gave her a kiss goodbye. Nothing fancy but enough to let her know that I wanted to see her again.

On the way home, I felt that rush of happiness that you have when you know you have just experienced something unique. I felt like a teenager again. I also felt the urge to pick up the phone and give Gina a call. I didn't want to seem too excited by calling her too soon, but something inside me said, "Do it."

"Hi," I said when she picked up on the other end. "I just wanted to say again it was great seeing you and hope we can do this again soon." I knew I was repeating what I'd said to her in the parking lot, but isn't it true that you never get a second chance at a second chance? I would later find out from Gina that she also felt the same way—she had wanted to reach out to me on the drive home but didn't want to seem overzealous, so when she saw my name come up on the car display, she couldn't believe it. She said she was so happy, there were tears in her eyes when she answered and heard my voice. That's the power of face-to-face interaction—we both knew there was something more once we had met up after so many years.

Over the next few months, we saw each other regularly. We talked about our past, our present—and our future. Gina was living in southern New Jersey in Cherry Hill, and I was living in Long Beach, New York, so the typical drive was a minimum of two hours. At first, our relationship was a logistical challenge, but the relationship was growing, and seeing each other was key to its growth. I often left early on Fridays on weekends when I wasn't seeing my kids, and the occasional surprise visit during the week started to become routine.

As our relationship grew, two moments spoke volumes to me. On one of our earlier dates, we had dinner in an Italian restaurant in Staten Island, and as we were leaving the restaurant, we were saying our goodbyes. Gina had her back against the brick wall outside of the restaurant, and I knew something special would happen. For me, it was the look of her blue eyes locked with mine. And then my lips met hers, and my hand touched the side of her face, and her hand reached the back of my neck, gently pulling me close. Something about the kiss said, "I want more." To me, the kiss is one of the most electrifying experiences between a man and a woman. I agree with Albert Einstein, who said, "Any man who can drive safely while kissing a pretty girl is simply not giving the kiss the attention it deserves." (Who am I to argue with a Nobel prize winner?) The kiss tells you about your partner's passion and, to me, is the doorway to the soul. At that moment, I felt I was introduced to Gina's soul. That kiss let me know that there was something very special going on between us.

The next somewhat ordinary moment that told me our relationship was going somewhere special occurred at a Starbucks in New Jersey after we had been seeing each other for about six months. It was a warm, sunny day, so we took our coffee to the outdoor sitting area and sat down to enjoy a little time together. Gina's dog, Yussel, a Wheaten terrier, laid down on the pavement at Gina's feet and watched everyone walk by.

Gina and I just sat there chatting about movies we had recently seen and other small talk when it dawned on me: This moment, right here and right now, was one of the best I've ever had. I was sitting with a woman whom I was falling in love with, simply having a cup of coffee, and I was completely enthralled. The sharing, the authenticity and bonding, turned that ordinary cup of coffee into an extraordinary cup of coffee.

That moment was the start of taking the simplest things in life and elevating them to a higher plane—it was the beginning of creating extraordinary events from ordinary moments of life. My brother had tried to tell me about this feeling when he said, "All I need is a bagel, coffee, and the beach," but it wasn't until I spent time with Gina that I truly grasped the concept. For us, it was a glass of wine, a cup of coffee, breakfast outdoors, a walk on the boardwalk, or a bicycle ride.

SHARING SOMETHING VERY SIMPLE WITH SOMEONE ELSE IN YOUR LIFE CREATES A SYNERGY THAT IS UNIQUE AND PROFOUND.

The truth is most of us are used to defining "extraordinary" as something way beyond the normal—something far bigger than mundane things in life, like drinking coffee. Of course a hot-air balloon ride over Napa Valley in California is extraordinary, but so is a walk on the beach. Even when you don't have a life partner, sharing something very simple with someone else in your life creates a synergy that is unique and profound.

When you grow up with nothing, you learn to appreciate everything. When you can't feed yourself, the lousiest sandwich becomes a three-course meal. When you are a child with no authentic relationships, an hour-long chat becomes the highlight of your month. The challenges that I faced as a teenager gave me a special power—the power to see ordinary moments as extraordinary. And that's how Gina and I have become so happy. When we're together, we focus on each other. And even if we're doing little, ordinary things, they become extraordinary—because we're together. Face-to-face.

For me, it was so nice to have someone who I really synced with, someone with whom I could share dreams and concerns and who helps to make each day better than the one before. I had really never experienced the level of harmony I found with Gina, a kind of equilibrium state with another human.

Once Gina's youngest daughter, Lana, left home to go to college, Gina moved back to New York. We moved to a townhouse together, and our kids all came to visit us regularly. I was so happy that I found myself pushing a little harder on the accelerator when coming home after work, just so that I could arrive sooner.

After several years of living together, we decided to get married. It simply made sense. We both have a spiritual side and believed it was something we ought to do—and I'm so glad that we did. After thirty-plus years of going our own way, we had reconnected so strongly that we both felt we were truly drawn together by something more divine.

From a more down-to-earth standpoint, Gina and I really seem to have a connection that allows us to be the best versions of ourselves. Communication is always key for us, and we really support each other, whether it's a career move, improving our health, or spiritual and mental growth. We also help our respective children try to be the best versions of who they are. Gina was there for my children, Matthew and Sari, when their mom passed away, and she has always tried to be there when they need her. Likewise, I have always made myself available for Gina's daughters, Jessica and Lana, when they need guidance and counsel or just simply someone to chat with. Our family is enriched by the four kids with very different personalities, each contributing to the success of a happy family.

From a different perspective what Gina and I have is really similar to a business partnership. Indeed, the common denominators are striking: trust, accountability, good communication, and, of course, success.

We are fully aware of each other's strengths and weaknesses, and when necessary, we constructively discuss areas that we may disagree on. For example, Gina is more financially conservative than I am, and her input has helped me save thousands of dollars when buying a car. When she has issues at work for which she needs suggestions, I give her my input, and she often finds it very helpful. It's really a partnership that continues to evolve, and it is without question why I continue to find success in all facets of my life, including business.

In fact, she helps me when things get a little stressful at work. She's great at bringing me back down to earth in a very logical, rational way by simply asking, "What's the worst that could happen?" which often turns into "That's really not that bad." Similarly, I help her when she needs an opinion about something that's going on in her work.

Our conversations often take on a life of their own, from the very deep and existential, like what happens after life, to why we both like black-and-white movies. And we laugh—regularly. I'll repeat—we laugh, regularly, with the vigor that almost makes you lose your breath. Her presence in my life rekindled a spiritual flame that I longed for. She is a talented musician who plays the guitar and sings as passionately as anybody I've heard. Sure, I'm biased, but isn't that what you're supposed to be to a certain extent when you've been blessed with this type of relationship?

I would be remiss in talking about my partner in life if I didn't discuss intimacy. First, intimacy doesn't always mean sex, although if you're not having regular sexual intimacy with your partner, unless it's based on medical issues, red flags should be going up. I believe sexual intimacy is key to keeping each other connected in a deep and spiritual way. Earlier, I mentioned how the kiss for me is an essential part of our connection. The right kiss at the right time sends a message to your partner's soul. It starts those moments of deep connection. Sure, I know that not every moment of physical intimacy needs to send you to the stars—but then, maybe it should.

Without regular physical intimacy, resentment, anger, and negative emotions will eventually be part of your everyday feelings. You know what happens next? An implosion within the partnership, and that is not good for anyone's life. Physical intimacy also consists of simple moments like a hug, a shoulder rub, a look in the eyes, and, yes, the kiss. The bottom line is to create regular intimacy, regardless of how busy you are. Have dinner together—just the two of you. Once again, many of the characteristics that I've shared with you about creating authentic and genuine relationships would apply to this deep and unique bond.

IN-PERSON, FACE-TO-FACE CLOSENESS MAKES ALL THE DIFFERENCE. IT IS ESSENTIAL FOR ANY HIGHLY COVETED RELATIONSHIP THAT IS IMPORTANT TO YOUR SUCCESS—IN LIFE OR IN BUSINESS.

I'll say it again: In-person, face-to-face closeness makes all the difference. It is essential for any highly coveted relationship that is important to your success—whether personal or business. Any relationship needs its own form of oxygen, and to breathe life into it requires a physical connection.

For instance, when I meet somebody, not only do I shake their hand but also, when we get up from our chairs and are laughing and talking, I might put my hand on their shoulder because physicality is extremely important to me. To me, it translates to a message of genuine caring and concern if it's done authentically.

Yes, digital is important in our world today. And keeping in touch through phone calls is also important when distance keeps you apart. But genuine relationships are made stronger by the human touch. I think many of us have learned that now that we've been through a point in our history when we had to refrain from physical contact. Thanks to digital, we were still able to see each other through the pandemic. We're able to begin business relationships by connecting on LinkedIn. But nothing replaces a handshake. Nothing replaces sitting across the table from someone over a business lunch—or a cup of coffee.

While texting Gina was fun, we would never have rekindled our teenage romance if we hadn't met face-to-face. We would never have married. Now that we are married, it's the face-to-face time that keeps the magic alive. It all goes back to making the ordinary extraordinary through simple acts like sitting with a cup of coffee and talking or taking a walk on the beach.

Whether you're making a new friend, talking to a new client, or falling in love, you can't afford to let technology get in the way. Social media is a great way to initiate a connection, as I've experienced firsthand, but it's no way to deepen one.

Invest in people face-to-face and you will reap the rewards for a lifetime.

ACTIONABLE SUCCESS MOVES

▷ Set aside regular times to meet your most important relationship partners.

▷ Reconnect with old relationships, even those that may have ended badly. More often than not, these connections will turn out to be positive.

▷ Are you and your spouse or life partner accountable to each other? Are you accountable to each other not only at home but also for each other's jobs, whether you are working at home or outside of the home?

▷ Write down one trait that you and your partner or spouse have that is stronger than the others (e.g., she's great with money and I'm not).

▷ When creating new relationships, remember your body: shaking hands, making eye contact, giving pats on the back, and even hugging when appropriate. If that's not who you are, then take a small step with just one of these with someone you're comfortable with.

▷ Write down three things you and your spouse/partner do that are SAFE— simple, alone, free (or inexpensive), and extraordinary.

CHAPTER 6

BUILDING BRIDGES
THE POWER OF FINDING COMMON GROUND

*I've learned that people will forget what you said, people will forget
what you did, but people will never forget how you made them feel.*
—MAYA ANGELOU

On some level, the behaviors in the previous chapters all contain some
element of the behavior in this chapter: finding common ground. In
order to create authentic, trustful, genuine relationships, you've got to
find some common ground, and that comes from finding your people,
acknowledging the need for others, listening more than you talk, and
making face-to-face contact.

As a recap, in chapter 2 I talked about how I didn't have naturally
strong relationships growing up, so I had to build relationships inten-
tionally as a teen. Chapter 3 revealed that building strong relationships
requires us to first acknowledge how important those relationships

are—that our lives are far more enriched with the help and presence of other people. Chapter 4 was about the importance of listening more than talking. If you don't listen to someone, you won't be able to understand where they're coming from, and if you don't understand where a person is coming from, you can never really connect with them. Chapter 5 was about the power of time spent face-to-face and how ordinary moments can become extraordinary when you really value that in-person quality time.

But even if you know you need others, you listen more than you talk, and you meet with people face-to-face, in order to build deep, lasting relationships, you must be able to relate to the other person. That takes finding something you have in common—that's the glue that binds together the other behaviors into a relationship-building talent. You won't always find that common ground right away, and once you do, sometimes you have to nurture it. But once you have it, that really solidifies the relationship.

IF YOU'RE UNABLE TO CONNECT WITH OTHERS IN A MEANINGFUL WAY, THEN YOU'RE LIMITING SUCCESS IN ALL AREAS OF YOUR LIFE.

Although I had begun to learn how to find my people and build relationships as a teen, it was actually during my college years that I started forming really deep connections with people—connections rooted in common interests, values, and temperaments. Being involved with others certainly brought a level of gratification. But I've always felt that our society places a much heavier emphasis on academics and expanding one's intellectual capacity. I believe you need a mix of both, because you can be the student with the best grades, but if you're unable to connect with others in a meaningful way, then you're limiting success in all areas of your life.

So once I had my GED, I pursued a new opportunity to reinvent myself—higher education. I started by attending Nassau Community College, a two-year college that I commuted to. Compared to larger colleges or universities with on-campus housing, there were somewhat limited opportunities to get involved outside of the classroom. Nevertheless, I still wanted to try to recreate or build on the experiences I had when I was with the B'nai B'rith Youth Organization.

My initial career objective was to work in the healthcare arena because of my experiences with my mother's health. I wasn't sure exactly what area of healthcare but initially thought it would be physical therapy or some other allied health profession.

I entered college with a new level of confidence, having been through the B'nai B'rith experience and worked several different jobs by then. I knew what it was like to speak to other people my age, to mix with people who were smarter than me and who came from different socioeconomic backgrounds and yet feel comfortable with them all—and in my own skin.

But having dropped out of high school, I found myself retreating back to my old, dark feelings of who I was in the world and feeling, quite frankly, a bit overwhelmed by the college scene. In my mind, everyone there had an edge over me since they had been in a school environment for the past few years, and I was coming equipped with only a GED. Some of the old self-doubts started to creep in, but I knew I had to do something to continue building new relationships. Even though I was a dropout, I was not intellectually bankrupt, and I felt I had matured at a much more rapid pace than other kids—I had to.

But I essentially missed the opportunity to be an adolescent; whereas in high school, most kids are playing out that role of the teenager, I didn't really get the chance to do all those things. I never really felt a commonality with anyone back then until I underwent a transformation with B'nai B'rith. That helped propel my confidence and feeling that I belonged to a group, and some of that still remained with me. So college was really taking a chance at getting past those feelings that had led me to drop out of high school.

Once I started to get the hang of things, my confidence began to improve. I'd get a good grade that made me feel like I wasn't dumb or a failure, so I would try another challenge and then another.

As a way of connecting with other like-minded people, I decided to form a club on campus. I thought I would be able to meet with other people who were in similar situations, other students in the allied health field. I was friendly with the chair of the health education department who was also the professor of the sex education class I was in. When I approached her about forming a club, she was more than willing to help me. A year later, she wrote a letter of recommendation for me that I still have; in it, she referred to me as someone who "would not settle for mediocrity." I was humbled by her words and still treasure that letter to this day.

With her help, I was able to form a group called the Health Awareness Society. At first, I was the founder and president of a group that had only one member—me. Looking back, I thought everyone likely knew I was a high school dropout; they probably detected it from the corny name that I gave the group. It certainly didn't have a "college-sounding" name to it. I put up flyers around campus, and the professors made announcements in various classes, but no one wanted to join, or so I thought.

At the time, there was a radio talk show that was growing in popularity in the New York area. It featured a woman named Dr. Ruth Westheimer who was quickly becoming a phenomenon by revolutionizing discussions about health and sexuality. A very short, tiny woman with a heavy German accent, who at the time was in her sixties, Dr.

Ruth, as she was affectionately called, was candid and funny about the subject of sex—and college kids loved her. I called her and left a message on her answering machine: "Would you consider talking to my group?" Part of me hoped she wouldn't respond because there was no group yet. Unbelievably, she did get back to me, and even more incredibly, she agreed to come and talk to our group.

Immediately I went into high gear. There was no social media back then, so, once again, I passed out flyers all over the campus. Can you guess what happened? That's right, within a few days, I had a list of names of students who wanted to join the group that I had formed. I guess Dr. Ruth was the draw that I needed. Later on, I found out that others had wanted to join at the outset but were embarrassed or just too shy.

Dr. Ruth's visit was a success, and so was the group, which ultimately met weekly. I came to know a lot of really nice people through that group, and we talked every week about something we all had a passion for—health.

I've always believed that joining groups is a great way to build relationships. More than just the professional associations or opportunities to network or add a prestigious title to your résumé, however, I'm a fan of getting involved in groups you have a genuine affinity for, something that can help you create authentic relationships. Don't join a pediatric cancer foundation just because you think it's the cool organization to be part of now; while a very honorable type of organization, you should join only if you have a genuine or vested interest. When I joined the National Multiple Sclerosis Society, I had a vested interest in it because that was the illness that took my mother from me, and I didn't want to see other families go through that. Trust me, if you join a group just for the prestige or for some business networking, you won't come across as authentic, and your lack of interest will be apparent. Get involved in something you really have a passion for, and you're going to find and build authentic relationships.

Over the next four years, I went to four different colleges and universities, all with their own unique tilt. As I shared in chapter 3, after I graduated from community college, I went to Baruch College in New York City as the start of my pursuit of a bachelor's degree, then went to State University of New York (SUNY) at Albany, which was my first experience at living away from home—something I always thought was for the few and privileged.

By the time I entered Albany, my career path had evolved. While I wanted to help people like my mother with physical ailments and chronic health issues, I didn't feel that healthcare allowed me to advocate in the manner that I wanted to. I wanted to work for so many others who were also the underdog. I wanted to help those who were afflicted with physical challenges to regain their sense of dignity and self-worth. But I also wanted to be there for people who were placed in horrible situations through no fault of their own.

I was working on a bachelor's degree in political science when law captured my attention, so while at Albany, I began getting involved with clubs for students who wanted to go to law school. Living on campus also allowed me to make deeper and longer-lasting relationships, some of which became lifelong relationships.

One of my most treasured friendships at the time was with Irwin, who came from the Bronx and modest beginnings. He was truly the type of friend I could relate to. During school, his father passed away, and when he came back from being home with his family, Irwin and I sat outside, and I listened to him for a bit—that's when I first discovered that we had a connection that would last well beyond our college years. Another friend, Neil, who I originally met in B'nai B'rith, was also in Albany, and we ultimately shared an apartment off campus.

When you're away at school, there is more "living" time with other people, and you begin to see the things you have in common with the rest of your peers far more intensely than the differences. Neil became a high-powered attorney, and we still stay in touch.

Some of the relationships I made, both in and out of school, have turned out to be long term, although intermittent. Take Larry, for instance, a very close childhood friend whose family moved to Texas. Our relationship continued at first but then dwindled to a few conversations over the next twenty years. After my divorce, we rekindled that friendship, and since then we've visited each other several times and talk on the phone regularly. Just because a

> **SOME OF THE BEST, MOST LONG-LASTING RELATIONSHIPS WILL GO THROUGH CYCLES, GETTING STRONGER ALONG THE WAY.**

relationship doesn't serve its purpose at a certain moment in your life doesn't mean it can't be rekindled at another point when it makes sense for both of you. And relationships don't always have to be fifty-fifty. Sure, there should be some give and take, but sometimes a relationship is more give, sometimes more take, and that's okay. Some of the best, most long-lasting relationships will go through cycles, getting stronger along the way.

While away from home attending school at Albany, finances took hold of my life again, and I finished my bachelor's degree at Queens College. Although it was a commuter school, it was loaded with extra-curricular activities, so there was no excuse not to get involved.

During my senior year, I also experienced extraordinary academic success. I was now discovering my writing skills as well as polishing the speaking skills that I started with at B'nai B'rith. I was involved in multiple debate and communication classes, which I not only did very well in but also actually enjoyed. I loved higher education, and to this day, when September rolls around, I long to go back to school and feel the excitement and energy that comes from learning and making new connections.

By the time I graduated, I had decided to attend law school, and I was preparing my life for that venture. I started working in the legal field in my junior year in college. I worked for smaller firms where creating relationships was not only easier but also essential. It was during this time that I started to turn inward and began to use my strengths in forming authentic and trustful relationships in business.

As I mentioned earlier, I applied to several very good law schools. I was limited by finances, which required me to attend school at night since I had to work during the day. I was prepared to go anywhere that would accept me and felt the law school gatekeepers (admissions counselors) would see me as second rate because of my high school dropout status. In the end, I was accepted to every law school I applied to and ultimately decided to attend New York Law School in downtown New York because it was walking distance to my law clerk job, about ten blocks away.

I knew that if I had to go to law school at night, I would never be the A student; I had to accept that. I knew I would push myself enough to pass but not enough to graduate top of the class. I mean, think about the math here. Eight to nine hours at work, evening classes start anywhere from six to seven o'clock and would typically end between eight and ten. Going home was an hour-and-a-half journey. If you're any kind of normal human being, you need seven to eight hours of sleep. Add it up. Where is the study time? Where is the time to eat?

Yes, there were many students who were able to pull it off, but I wasn't one of them. I knew that my objective was to learn as much as I could and meet as many people as I could. Many of my classmates were older than me and were working in various professions, from nursing to law enforcement. My goal was to survive and take the bar exam and pass. It was also to meet more people and create an even larger circle of trusted relationships. Indeed, I still keep in close contact with a few of those classmates, and I consider them wonderful, genuine, and authentic friends.

But I almost blew it in the first semester. I received a letter in the mail that no first-year student wants—a warning notice putting me on probation because my first semester grades fell below a 2.0. Maybe it was the brief summer break between graduating with my bachelor's degree and starting law school the next semester. For me, I guess that summer break was too much of a breather from constant challenges; I gained a sense of confidence that I could handle it all without much effort. I hadn't prepared myself physically and mentally for how much law school and working would tax my capacity—I wasn't ready when life came knocking. Another life-teaching moment: Never underestimate the challenge and never overestimate your ability. In other words, don't become complacent—when you underestimate the challenge, you don't give it your all.

In law school, the professors really hold you accountable. The first evening that I was in contracts class with Professor James Brooks, a very serious and intimidating instructor who looked the professorial part, he wanted to go over the assignment that everyone had to read (some old English case). Since it was a class of one hundred students, I thought for sure he would never call on me, so I simply didn't do the reading in advance. The first person he called was the young lady sitting right next to me. Her response: "I'm sorry, I didn't read the case." He said nothing, so I figured I was safe—surely he wouldn't call on the person sitting right next to her. But as he looked over his list of student names, I realized he had no idea who was sitting where.

When he next called out, "Neal Goldstein," I broke into a sweat. How the hell could this happen to me? I figured I would say the same thing that she said—"I'm sorry, I didn't read the case"—and wait for him to react with silence as he had with the first student. But I knew I was in trouble when he slowly removed his glasses. "You have a responsibility to the class, to me, and to yourself," he said. Boy, did that stick! Needless to say, I was prepared for every contracts class and actually came to like Professor Brooks. By the way, the girl sitting next to me? She became a judge.

I knew pretty soon after entering law school that I wanted to be the lawyer for people whose lives were disrupted and often destroyed by circumstances beyond their control. My law clerk job was with a personal injury firm, and through it, I found myself talking with many people whose life situations reminded me of my own. I found myself really relating to those people on so many different levels; most of them were truly genuine. When a member of the family is physically challenged, or worse, their life is devastated through no fault of their own, it's one of the most difficult things that a person—a whole family—can go through. Some of the experiences even gave me flashbacks to when I was helping my mom, for instance, by appearing before administrative agencies to obtain benefits for her.

I began to feel like personal injury was an area where I could really do well and help people. Why not use my own experiences and my knowledge of the law to help people better their lives or try to recoup what they had lost through no fault of their own?

At the end of the second year of law school, my classmates and I were gathered outside a classroom, and a question was going around the group: "What kind of law do you want to go into?" The answers came pretty rapidly: securities, contracts, corporate, and other high-falutin career choices. Don't get me wrong, those are all noble legal paths to take. But I was the only one to say personal injury. Standing there in that group and professing it out loud, I knew at that moment what I wanted, and I stayed focused from then on.

One of the great disadvantages I had in law school became a secret weapon. What I thought was a weakness or vulnerability—having to work during the day and sacrificing top grades—became a source of true strength. The lawyer I worked for was one of the fastest-growing firms in the area of personal injury.

As soon as I was hired as a law clerk, I was thrown into the fire, so to speak. I began working in all areas of litigation, and in addition to regular client contact, I also routinely went to the courthouse. Some of the things I was tasked with doing were borderline for a law student. For instance, one time I was sent to the courthouse in the Bronx to represent the firm and was in a conference with a judge and three other lawyers who were on the other side of the case. I acknowledged to the judge, because I felt that I had to, that I was not a lawyer and that I was still just a law student. Her look made me shrink back, and after she excused me, I got up from my chair and nearly ran out of the room (feeling about three feet tall).

Over four years I got to know adversarial lawyers, court clerks, and judges. I liked them and they liked me. Judges knew that I was in law school, many of them knew my background, and they all tried to give me their own bit of advice. Clerks always had a smile when I came into their courtroom. We would talk about sports, family, and sometimes the judges they worked for. In many ways, it was training that gave me a very competitive edge—most of my fellow students who had the luxury of going to school during the day or those who were fully occupied and going to school at night didn't have those opportunities that I had as a law clerk. That's just one reason why one of my mantras is that you must find your perceived disadvantage and leverage it.

Once I received my law degree, I began interviewing for jobs as a lawyer. That's when I learned something else about myself: I was really good at interviewing and ultimately getting offers. It almost became a hobby. I'd find out with whom I was interviewing and tried to get as much information on that person to see if we shared something in common. Maybe it was sports or where we lived or even a judge or clerk who I learned they had some contact with. I always listened to them and followed up on our conversations. I always tried to steer the discussion to their family or to something of interest. The lawyers were always impressed with my depth of knowledge of and experience with courtrooms, judges, and court clerks—especially for someone my age. They were equally impressed with "my story," which I often shared. As I'll explain more in-depth in the next chapter, the purpose in sharing my story in a conversation with a client is to let someone else know about struggles and challenges that they, too, can relate to. It also sends the message that I trust them enough to share my story. It without a doubt has helped me nurture these relationships beyond what most lawyers can ever have. Although I wasn't being offered attorney positions with white-shoe law firms, that really wasn't what I wanted. Instead, offers rolled in from the litigation firms that I interviewed with.

When I was working as a law clerk while in school, the firm that I was with was also quite impressed by how many clients I was able to bring in. I always wanted to let people know who I was and what kind of work I had done—from my mother's home health aide to taxi driver, bartender, and barber. And I let them know that now I was working in law, and if they needed me, to give me a call. Eventually I started getting the calls, and when I left that firm to find my first position as an attorney, I immediately had approximately fifty clients. That was unheard of as a student/law clerk unless you were poaching existing clients of the firm, which I would never do.

Ultimately, in 1991, I went to work as an associate for a long-standing but smaller litigation firm in downtown Manhattan. As an associate, I had my hands in everything from initial investigation of a claim to conducting depositions and even some trial work. Of course, what I truly loved was meeting and talking to prospective new clients and explaining to them how the legal system works and how I'd like to stand with them as they navigate the challenges of an often confusing, onerous, and overburdened system. The people who I have met and represented over the years have come from all walks of life. I've represented the rich and the poor; nurses, doctors, police offices, and firemen; teachers and students; moms and dads. And they all share one thing in common: They've allowed me to be their advocate through this legal maze, and in turn I've shown them respect and given them my undivided attention when they needed it. Period. There is no other way to be successful than to treat your clients with that standard of care.

Take, for instance, Josh, a young man who was in middle school and entering high school when he was bullied beyond comprehension. He had been stabbed with pencils in his stomach, kicked in his back until he was urinating blood, thrown on the sidewalk and beaten, and called the most vile words you can think of. His goal was to commit suicide at home on Christmas. His parents, two wonderful veterans, asked if I could help. I have a soft spot for younger kids, so I often get calls from parents about their child's bullying, and I am able to talk to most of them about how to resolve the issues without hiring me.

In Josh's case, his parents pleaded with the school numerous times to help protect their son, but their words fell on deaf ears. In fact, the school districts in these types of cases often try to blame the victim. This case was one that I had to handle. Before I was retained, however, I talked to Josh with his parents and then alone. We talked about his life and what he wanted to do, and I shared pieces of my life as well. When I told him my story, you could see that he immediately felt a special connection with me. Sure, different stories but struggles nonetheless. He knew he could call me anytime, with or without his parents present.

We appeared on radio and television, and I was so proud of how he held himself together. You couldn't help but root for this kid. After several years of litigation, we came to a settlement with the school district.

Later, I asked Josh what his plans were, and he told me he wanted to go into the US Air Force. His mom also told me later that I helped save her son's life. Their words meant everything to me. Yes, I had been paid for my services, but that was nothing compared to hearing Josh tell me of his plans for the future and his mother's gratefulness that her son would live a full life. That's the true value I get from what I do.

From helping victims, I get to develop real, authentic, and genuine friendships. In another case, my team and I helped Bernice, a sweet elderly woman who was a passenger in an accident in which the car she was in overturned, resulting in a severe degloving injury to her arm. Degloving means that the top layer of skin and tissue is ripped from the underlying muscle. A very serious injury for anyone, let alone a senior. I called Bernice regularly to check on her and see if she was okay and how she was doing. We got to know each other very well. She was a woman of tremendous wisdom. I learned about her life and family. We still talked after her case was resolved, and though she since passed, I still talk to her family, including her son, with whom I have lunch several times a year.

> *It's fascinating how the fundamentals of business-to-business marketing are the same today as they were fifty years ago. It's still about relationships.*
> **—DAVID MEERMAN SCOTT**

Finding common ground with clients and with others whom I work with in this field has been the key to my success. In court, when arguing a case before a judge, I may not be as refined as the other lawyer, and they may be able to express the rule of law better than me. But no one gets as emotional as I do. No one can express to the judge the client's suffering better than I can. Sometimes the judge has even had to tell me, "Okay, Counselor, calm down. I understand what you're saying"—that's how passionate I am when I've connected to a client and their situation. And the judge can see that—if I tried to be more like the other lawyer, it wouldn't be authentic, and the judge wouldn't feel the connection.

Likewise, I carry my passion even after the client's matter is resolved. A client who I had, Linda, whose matter had been resolved, called me one day to tell me that her husband—someone whom I really liked—had passed away. The client, understandably, had been having a hard time with the grieving. I felt she really needed someone to talk to, so I asked her if she would join me for lunch, which she did a few weeks later. I can't tell you how good she felt that someone, let alone her former lawyer, would take her to lunch simply to chat and take her mind off the loss that she was experiencing, if only for an afternoon. That's how to build true connections with other human beings: empathy and compassion in times of need.

I want the members of my team to also feel a sense of connection with clients and others whom we work with. I want them to truly understand where a client is coming from so that their relationship with the client can be that much stronger. It's more than just superficial knowledge about a case, such as "This client was in a car accident." It's the fact that the client was in a car accident, this is how the accident happened, and now he's in the hospital and out of work, and he has a wife and children at home who he needs to support. When they really understand a client's situation, it creates a new dynamic when they are working with them—for instance, their questions are more targeted and demonstrate genuine concern. That helps solidify the relationship not only between my team and our clients but also between the client and me. The team is always an extension of who I am.

In my office, we don't wait for clients to call us. We reach out to them to see how they are doing. We use a system I developed called HAY—How Are You? Every few weeks, we reach out and ask, "How are you?" In the US, one of the top complaints by clients is that no one ever calls back. We employ the HAY system to get ahead of clients' concerns. We build such strong relationships with clients that it's not uncommon for them—and us—to truly feel a bit sad when a case is over. That's how strong the relationships are.

I've been a lawyer for over thirty years, and for most of that time, I've owned a personal injury law firm. During that period of time, my firm has represented almost five thousand clients and has successfully resolved hundreds of millions of dollars' worth of cases. By all accounts, the numbers make it appear that we've done very well. But the real value can't be quantified in numbers. It's the kind words, the beautiful letters that have been written to me, and the reviews my firm continues to get about how well we treat our clients and how we respect each of our clients regardless of the value of their case. Most importantly, it's the messages and comments that we get that let us know we're being authentic.

Though I enjoyed litigation and advocating for my clients in court, conducting thousands of depositions questioning everyone from negligent drivers to neurosurgeons, I've now pivoted to helping people in another way. These days, I prefer taking the time to nurture client relationships in greater depth, so communication is more accessible and understandable to the client. This is essential today more than ever, with the thousands of mixed messages from social media from all kinds of pundits, including many lawyers.

For me, the relationship with the client (especially at the outset) is and always will be the key. So instead of pursuing trial techniques or becoming an expert on the law behind personal injury work, I decided to focus on building relationships with people I could relate to. And, in the long run, that decision made me successful because it put me on a path toward developing deep relationships with my clients and my professional peers. Frankly, that has helped me grow as a person as well.

By sharing this book with you, I've now pivoted once again to helping other people who want to succeed in their lives through the power of authentic and genuine relationships.

I owe all of my success to the power of common ground. People don't choose me as their attorney because I'm a world-famous litigator. They choose me because I'm deeply committed to authenticity. They choose me because they see themselves in me, and I see myself in them as well.

That's the power of finding common ground: it creates trust and instant connection, and it's an essential component of every deep, rewarding relationship.

ACTIONABLE SUCCESS MOVES

▷ Get involved in organizations or groups that focus on things that you love or feel passionately about. Don't think of it as a business lead generator, though it will be one day.

▷ We all have at least one weakness, and many of us have more than one. Write a paragraph on yours. Review the paragraph two days later. Do you still feel the same way? Ask someone close to you if they see it as a weakness. Often, our perceived weakness is defined very differently by others and in fact may be a source of strength.

▷ Follow the **How Are You?** (HAY) system in whatever business you are in to develop the kind of relationships that will create true success. Call your clients/customers and ask them how they are doing. This can vary in methods depending on your business. (I don't expect my pizza place to call and ask me how I'm doing, but then again, why not?) Sometimes it's a phone call or simply a free entrée because I'm a regular customer.

CHAPTER 7

SHARE YOUR STORY
ONCE UPON A TIME ...

There comes a point in your life when you need to stop reading other people's books and write your own.
—ALBERT EINSTEIN

One of the hardest moments of my life was the day I told my mother I was dropping out of high school. She was sitting in her wheelchair in her bedroom, and I walked in and handed her a consent form to sign acknowledging that I was dropping out of school. "I'm dropping out," I told her matter-of-factly. That moment was all the harder because my mom couldn't fight me; when you're going through your own personal hell, you don't have the strength to argue. She held her hand to her forehead in what appeared to be a moment of surrender, then, using her left hand because she had limited use of her dominant right hand, she signed. Her signature looked like something a child would scrawl.

That scene often replays in my mind, a reminder of the anguish that I caused in that moment. As a parent today, I still feel at times that it was unforgivable. That moment has become one of the most important scenes (along with a few others) in the story of my life. In the last chapter, we spoke about the importance of finding commonalities, and that moment is often one that people relate to. Not everybody was a high school dropout, and not everybody had a mother who went through what mine did, but we've all experienced what it is to let someone down. And for many of us, we know what it is to disappoint a parent or to feel neglected by one.

Throughout this book, I've talked about my life and the lessons learned on that journey. That's one way of demonstrating another very powerful way to find common ground when building relationships—learn to share your story. When you discover your story and share it in a genuine and authentic way, it shows. Even though it changes over time, when you open yourself up to others in a truthful way—not a way to try to manipulate the situation—then people will be drawn to you as someone who is honest and genuine. When trying to create authentic, trustful relationships, sharing a part of your journey is one of the most important things to do well.

WHEN YOU DISCOVER YOUR STORY AND SHARE IT IN A GENUINE AND AUTHENTIC WAY, IT SHOWS.

Admittedly, it was tough to really dig deep and to come up with the right words for some of what I've shared. Sometimes it takes real reflection to discover your story before you can share it. One way to discover your story, I've found, is to create prompts—simple questions that will help you remember things from your past that you've tucked away and don't think about anymore. If you respond to those prompts, coming up with some answers, then you'll start putting together the puzzle of your story. A prompt might be something like "Tell me about a birthday that you celebrated when you were younger," "Tell me about your best friend in college," "Where did you go on your last trip?" "What's your favorite meal?" Whether you say that to yourself or to someone else, it will spark a memory or an experience or a moment. Once you start putting the answers to those prompts together, you'll find that you'll begin remembering a lot of things that you haven't thought about in a while, and soon you'll have a "script," a story about yourself, about your journey.

For many years I denied how the script that had played out before me had any real consequences in my life. I simply shoved the entire childhood and adolescent period to the side and told myself I was doing okay. I remember sitting at a girlfriend's house for dinner and her mother being so impressed at how much I achieved considering my background; I kept saying to her, "Yes, thankfully it didn't affect me." I didn't know it at that point, but clearly the challenges in my life affected me significantly. By trying to always improve who I was and where I wanted to be, I was able to start being comfortable with myself. That helped me begin to look back at my life's journey, which ultimately helped me to move forward, something I've always associated with driving a car. When driving, where do you focus? On the windshield, the road ahead. No need to keep looking in the rearview mirror, but that doesn't mean never looking back. If you're always looking back, you're going to crash. But it's important to understand where you've been in order to guide where you want to go and, conversely, where you don't want to go. In fact, one of the most memorable and impressionable commencement speeches I've ever heard was from Steve Jobs, in which he said,

You can't connect the dots looking forward; you can only connect them looking backward. So you have to trust that the dots will somehow connect in your future. Because believing that the dots will connect down the road will give you the confidence to follow your heart, even when it leads you off the well-worn path, and that will make all the difference.[1]

In looking back, I found that there were pieces of my life that needed to be acknowledged, but that doesn't mean they need to be lived in my own life today. My mother wasn't a great communicator, and my father lacked compassion, humanity, and integrity, and needless to say he was a terrible role model—those are cycles that I want to break. So I'm determined to have good relationships with my children, to be a good communicator and the best father I can be. When you look back, you can decide what you want to leave behind and what you want to bring forward. I'm telling my story, in part, because I want to be a good example for my children of what it means to face and overcome challenges because they can equip you for when life comes knocking. In losing their mother, they certainly know what it means to face—and navigate—challenge, and I hope one day they will be able to look back on that and realize that it helped to equip them with tools that they've been able to use throughout their lives.

We all have a story to tell: Many of us don't know our own story, many of us know our story but aren't willing to acknowledge it, and many of us know our story, acknowledge it, but are unwilling to share it. Yes, of course, you have every right to bury that story inside of you and not share it with anyone else. But you will never unlock your true

1   "Steve Jobs' 2005 Stanford Commencement Address," Stanford University YouTube channel, accessed March 6, 2022, https://www.youtube.com/watch?v=UF8uR6Z6KLc.

potential in whatever you do in life unless that story is shared with another human being. I'm not saying that you have to tell the world, like I'm doing. You don't have to reveal your deepest secret to someone you just met in order to gain their trust. That might even be seen as oversharing. But telling part of your story to someone else is the way to begin to build trust.

That's what it boils down to—trust. Some people are just very closed and very slow to trust others. But trust is like a bank account; the more you deposit into that account, the more it grows.

Let's say you've found someone who you feel you really want to have a relationship with, whether in your personal life or in business. One way to build that is by making a trust deposit—sharing an appropriate piece of your story that the other person doesn't know. When they hear that, they internalize, "This person is trusting me," and they start to trust you in return. For some people, it's a slow process—it's very hard to get them to loosen their own purse strings, to gain their trust. But over time, you'll find that the trust builds and the relationship grows stronger.

My own story was so much of a roller coaster of love, marriage, divorce, adverse health, insecurity, family deaths, and more that I ultimately decided to get a healthy dose of therapy.

I was lucky enough to have found a wonderful therapist who, through twenty years of treatment, helped me see that all of my experiences were part of my journey and to help me learn how to articulate the pieces until they all fit a narrative or story. My time with Ellen, my therapist on the upper west side of Manhattan, was an evolution in and of itself. At first I was quiet, and she patiently waited for me to begin the conversations. At times I hated the start of our sessions; I simply didn't know what to say. Finally, I realized it wasn't a situation in which I was there to talk about her; I was there to talk about me.

I was center stage, and I could say anything that was on my mind. I knew I was in the groove on those days when I walked in with one thing on my mind and began a discussion that evolved into a completely different topic. As an example, I would begin by wanting to talk about an argument with Vicki, and by the end of the session, I was wondering out loud what my father was doing. Yet it all made sense, and it helped me share my story. Thank you, Ellen.

Sharing your story is one of the few ways that people are ever going to find common ground with you. It's also one of the most powerful ways that you can help other people. Stories touch us and transform us. They help us connect to each other, and they help us learn from each other. No two people will have the same story, although there might be some similarities. That's what makes sharing your story so relevant to relationship-building. Plus, in the business world, there's no better marketing tool—because it's unique to you. As a reminder, when we share a piece of our story with another and it's done in an authentic way, not for underhanded and cunning purposes, then it is the key that opens the door to successful relationships on all levels. Nobody knows you better than you.

> **STORIES TOUCH US AND TRANSFORM US. THEY HELP US CONNECT TO EACH OTHER, AND THEY HELP US LEARN FROM EACH OTHER.**

Understanding the power of sharing your story is part of what motivated me to write this book.

At its core, the book is for my children—it's meant to be a guide to living a good life. My hope is that these stories will help my children learn what it takes to form life-changing relationships. For me, the legacy of offering stories and lessons learned for my children is something that can't be erased, and my wish is that this book becomes an indelible part of their lives and their children's lives.

In this book, I've tried to share how my goal has been to be the parent I wish I had:

- A parent who's deeply involved, because he needs his children

- A parent who listens more than he talks

- A parent who makes time for extraordinary face-to-face moments

- A parent who relates to and finds commonalities with his kids

- And a parent who can tell his story to his children, using his past to teach them how to have a better future

From as early as I can remember I wanted to have a family, with children as an integral part of my life. As I said earlier, I fell in love with my children from the moment I met them, and it's been the most gratifying experience of my life to watch them grow up.

Matthew was a great little boy. He was always well dressed, thanks to his mother, and has always had a contagious laugh, along with a vibrant personality. He was (and still is) stubborn, but his smile and laugh are infectious. When he was an infant, I always helped Matt go to sleep, and if he woke up in the middle of the night, to give his mom a break, I would often get up and go to him to try to help him get back to sleep. I remember walking around with him at 2:00 a.m. in the kitchen until he nodded off. As a father, those are the moments that you embrace because that's when real bonding occurs. When he got older, I often took him on weekend day trips to the city to see a museum, eat at an unusual restaurant, enjoy a fair, or just join me in my office. He loved basketball and baseball, and we went to plenty of games, but I wonder sometimes if he'll remember just how much he loved those moments.

You see, for Matt, playing baseball was simply about putting on the uniform, being with other kids, getting a hit, sliding into a base, and just having fun. For me, that wasn't enough. I wanted him to be an above-average player and constantly reminded him during the games what to do and what not to do. This from a guy who was no Mickey Mantle as a kid and who was really clueless when it came to giving tips about how to play well. Did I want to make up for what I lost out on as a kid? Did I want to be super proud of his sports skills? Either way, I caused him plenty of stress—to the point that he became reluctant to get involved with other activities, which hurt because I was willing to look inward and realize I made a mistake. Fortunately, I learned my lesson and started listening when he told me that he just wanted to have fun. We had a strong enough relationship that it withstood those difficulties and others because the seeds of trust were planted. He knew that those moments were not his dad and that I would always be there when times were challenging. When he decided to play basketball, I just let him have fun and enjoy his life—by then I knew (as my brother Cary had taught me) to keep it simple. That's how to make things extraordinary.

Matt went through a "trying to be cool" phase in middle school but quickly learned that just being himself was the coolest thing he could do. In high school, he was an above-average student, and after college he successfully found his passion in the world of finance. Whatever he does, Matt's smile, sense of humor, and wanting to keep close to family will help him succeed in life.

Sari, my daughter, was nicknamed "the miracle baby" by her mother after the manner in which she entered the world. Early on, it was clear she would always walk to her own beat, and she was fairly independent in handling her typical school-age issues on her own.

I didn't get to spend as much time with Sari as I would have liked when she was an infant, but we certainly made up for that during her high school and college years.

Sari has always been a physically lovable person who, at times, remains quiet—so she can be hard to read. But like her brother, Sari has her own unique sense of humor and a great laugh. Early on, she seemed to have better athletic skills than the rest of us, so Vicki and I decided that we wanted her to be involved in a sport. Sari gravitated to tennis and began playing regularly and ultimately played for the high school. Honestly, I never thought the game was too exciting until I had a vested interest in it. I always admired the tenacity that Sari had, going to practice every day even when she truly didn't want to go, and I believe that her rigorous schedule is helping her develop into a very disciplined, very special young woman.

Sari's younger years were challenged by an initially tumultuous divorce and then by the passing of her mother. I will also never forget seeing my daughter, at ten years old, so visibly upset because she was the only one of her friends whose parents were divorced. Support, love, and ultimately reality would set in when a few years later many of her friends' parents joined the divorce club. There was nothing I could say to ease her pain in either situation, so I just listened. That has helped our relationship so much more than me talking. In fact, I think that's one of the ways Sari and I have bonded—she knows that when she wants to talk, I am there for her. When it came time to go to college, she chose a university in the northeast where none of her friends have gone and has elected to create new relationships. To her credit, she did a fabulous job at pulling it all together in the middle of a global pandemic at age eighteen, meeting more people than most kids do in a "normal" first year.

Of course, having a blended family meant that I was blessed with two more children who have contributed so much to our lives. Both Jessica and Lana have such a sense of focus, intent, and love of sharing that it's impossible to not feel fortunate to have their presence in our lives.

While I'd like to think that I played a positive and pivotal role in both of my children's lives, admittedly, I have had to overcome some of my own inner challenges as a parent. The number one issue I had to remind myself of was that my children are not me. Indeed, they may never be me. In some ways they may be better than me. While I have always wanted the relationship with my children to be an unbreakable bond that would never weaken, that simply isn't how it works. The relationship any parent has with their children must be built like a bridge—with expansion joints—so that it doesn't just snap but sways when under stress. And just like a bank account, you must keep depositing trust seeds so that when a withdrawal has to be made, it can be done without leaving the account depleted.

One thing that is incredibly gratifying is hearing them learn and repeat my stories and referring back to my crucial life lessons in casual conversations. I hope that their own memories will help them navigate this world and that they can begin to find their story and share it with others. I have always tried to teach my children the need to build relationships in order to succeed—as siblings, friends, partners, professionals, and adults.

Do I still worry about my kids? You bet! But I also know that each of them has a set of tools and has shown that they can move ahead. Some of the tools I've tried to hand down to them, some have been shared in our blended family, some have been discovered through substantial losses that were no fault of their own. Yet they've been able to navigate their way forward; they know what it means to suffer or be challenged in a meaningful way and yet still appreciate life.

In the future, when they inevitably will have issues, whether financial, marital, health, or something lesser, they will be better prepared because they are equipped with the tools that they need to overcome challenges. Of course, it will be their responsibility to use those tools when they are needed. Most of us have some experience that has left an indelible mark on us that we can use as a tool for understanding life's challenges a bit better. My children's experiences have equipped them to lead a life in which they may well be better prepared than I was to enjoy the success that life can offer.

Only one of my own stories remains to be shared: the outcome of that beautiful summer morning back in 1989 when my mom, Cary, and I were taking a drive. It wasn't an aimless drive; we had an exciting destination to go to—my graduation from law school. After I picked them both up, we headed for the ceremony, anticipating a late arrival. What we didn't know was that, of all the days, we happened to be on the road the same day the annual Puerto Rican Day Parade was going on. Ultimately, we managed to navigate the streets of Manhattan, arriving a few minutes late at Lincoln Center. I pulled the car over, opened the passenger door for my mother, opened the trunk, took out her wheelchair, picked her up out of the car and sat her in the chair, and off we went. Cary wheeled her in while we rushed through the building. I pushed the doors open, saw my friends in their black gowns, and headed to my seat.

After some fancy speeches by elite judges and then another one from the dean, the reading of names finally began—the names of the New York Law School graduates of 1989. My mom was sitting in her wheelchair at the end of a row of chairs where Cary, Vicki, and her mom and dad were seated.

They called out my name, "Neal Andrew Goldstein," and I headed for the stage, heart pounding. I took my time and even swaggered a bit, then walked up the steps, shook the hands of the dean and the dignitaries, and with sweaty palms, accepted the empty envelope that represented the diploma, the JD, Juris Doctorate.

Before I left the stage, I turned to the audience, and I looked for my mom. When I saw her sitting there, I waved the envelope at her and smiled—and she smiled back, a great, beaming smile. As I stood with envelope in hand, I was quickly reminded of that tortuous moment when I handed her my dropout papers to sign and thought, "We made it through this, Mom." For me, storybook endings actually exist.

ACTIONABLE SUCCESS MOVES

▷ At this point in the book, you may have started to think about your own story (some people may refer to it as your why). If you're having some difficulty piecing your story together (remember, everyone has one), go to my website, truthinsuccess.com, and see my list of prompts that may help you start to connect all your dots.

▷ If you have the means, I would strongly suggest that you look into a good therapist (yes, I really believe most people could benefit) who will guide you through finding how you evolved into the person you are.

▷ If you know your story but feel like you want to keep it private, that's okay. However, if you're uncomfortable sharing your story, consider just relating a few pieces of it to a close friend, spouse, or close relative (remember, a person's story is often made up of dozens of stories). Tell them to listen and not to comment unless you ask or to comment only on specific points (such as how the ending made them feel).

▷ After you've shared your story (or parts of your story) with someone, write down what, if any, changes you see in your relationship over the days and weeks going forward.

▷ Finally, if you're looking to attract more clients, share parts of your story in an honest and meaningful way in a blog, social media post, or even a video. When done with sincerity, it is by far the best way of achieving long-lasting and trustful relationships.

CONCLUSION

Relationships have been the key to everything in my life—they're the reason I've found success as a family man, a businessman, a friend, a father, a lawyer, and a member of my community. I've also successfully achieved peace with my faith and spirituality, which I have incorporated into my life in a comfortable and meaningful way.

On my journey, I learned early on that you can't move ahead in life if you're alone. That lesson is the first step that a person must take in order to build deep, rewarding relationships.

I also learned that relationships are a two-way street. You have to take an interest not only in sharing about yourself but also in learning about others. You have to listen more than you talk.

In the digital age, it's reasonable that a person might think they can do this kind of deep listening over the internet. But deep relationship building is something that can only happen face-to-face. It might not seem particularly special to get a cup of coffee with a person, but there is an extraordinary power in the ordinary behavior of meeting people in person.

As you spend more time with people, it's important to find common ground, to discover where your experiences, values, perspectives, and inclinations intersect. You need to relate in order to have a relationship.

Finally, you have to learn to tell your story. Of all the ways to connect with others, the idea of sharing your story may be the most important. You have to learn to be vulnerable, to share yourself with other people. When I hear a religious figure or an orator or a motivational speaker tell their own genuine stories, I always connect with them. It's sharing a piece of their life with me. They're being honest and authentic with me, and that creates space for me to be honest and authentic with them.

Growing up poor and longing for quality relationships, dropping out of high school, thinking about where the next meal was coming from—these were not pleasant experiences. I don't remember them fondly, and I'm left with scars, but I wouldn't trade them for anything. They are in my rearview mirror now, and in looking back and seeing them in perspective, I'm able to connect the dots to see how it all unfolded.

OF ALL THE WAYS TO CONNECT WITH OTHERS, THE IDEA OF SHARING YOUR STORY MAY BE THE MOST IMPORTANT.

Ultimately, my pain became my power: my circumstances taught me how to make ordinary moments extraordinary, how to enjoy the simple moments in life, how to use my level of sensitivity to help strengthen others, and, most important of all, how to foster deep, rewarding connections with the people around me.

In the end, what I teach my children—and what I hope you have also discovered by reading this book—is that success should not be defined as the wealthiest or the smartest person in the room. It should not be defined as the number of Facebook friends or Instagram followers you have. If you can learn to be kind, and if you can learn to connect, then the world will be yours for the taking.

WHAT CAN I DO RIGHT NOW TO START A BETTER LIFE?

▷   If you are keeping your journal as I hope you are doing, then on a new page write in all caps "TO BE CONTINUED." Consider sharing your journal (or a portion of it) with someone as soon as today and record how your relationship with that person evolves over the next few days and weeks. Then repeat the sharing process until you see the magic of creating authentic and trustful relationships.

▷   Go to truthinsuccess.com to continue the dialogue on authentic relationship-building and your success.

▷   Follow me on Instagram and Facebook to share your thoughts with like-minded people.

▷   Most importantly, call, email, or text that one person who you long to reconnect with and say, "I've been thinking about you." Now. Don't wait.

"What if I fail?" The more profound question is, "What if I never fail?" Stop making excuses and start managing your fear.
—DAVID MEERMAN SCOTT

LET'S CONNECT

Like you, I'm on all the social platforms (@nealagoldstein) and sure, we could connect there—but do you know what I'd love? Send me an email at NealG@TruthInSuccess.com and share a part of your story with me.

In the meantime, I'd like to invite you to get a free copy of "3 Ways You're Sabotaging Your Success and How to Change Them." Simply go to https://truthinsuccess.com/truth/ and tell me where to send it!

Thank you so much for joining me on this journey we call life. I am honored that you chose to spend a part of your path with me.

All the best,
Neal

ACKNOWLEDGMENTS

None of us got to where we are alone. Whether the assistance we received was obvious or subtle, acknowledging someone's help is a big part of understanding the importance of saying thank you.
—HARVEY MACKAY

So here I am writing a book about the importance of genuine relationships in our lives. Now I am sitting trying to collect my thoughts on thanking people who had an instrumental role in supporting me. Well, quite frankly, that could be another book. So, where do you begin, and more importantly, where do you end?

So let me start with the apology. I have been blessed to have so many good people in my life that there is simply no way to name them all here. My life has taken so many turns, and so many people have contributed to my success and well-being, that I simply won't be able to remember every person. So, if you are one of those people reading this and your name is not here, I apologize.

There are few words that I can say about my mother that I haven't said in the book. Nothing would be more fulfilling than to hug her one last time and say, "Thank you for never giving up and for always believing in me." Her smile, strength, and stamina in the middle of one firestorm after another redefined, for me, what courage is.

I would have never finished this project without my wife Gina's continuous and unconditional support. She finds my soul every day through a laugh, a piece of advice, or her loving words of encouragement. Thank you for allowing me to repeatedly read parts of the manuscript aloud, even when you were tired and simply wanted to watch *Jeopardy!* You always listen with love, compassion, and thoughtfulness. You've made me a better man.

To my children, Matt and Sari: the original idea was a legacy for you to share with your families, and you have generously allowed me to share this with others who may learn from these stories. To my stepchildren, Jessica and Lana: thank you for being who you are and for sharing yourselves and enriching my life so that we can have even more loving and genuine relationships.

I would simply be remiss if I didn't thank those who extended their hand to me in my younger years. Those that made me feel comfortable when all I felt was uncomfortable and those that attempted to talk to me with compassion and respect when I had no one else to talk to.

My childhood friends are still my friends today. Michael Auerbach and Andrew Fudrini made it possible for me to have some laughs when laughing wasn't easy. Larry Giordonello and his parents Ruth and Mark, who always made me comfortable in their home and who watched over Larry and me when we went on our first solo trip to Florida. Robin Reimer and her mom, Libby, who shared their kitchen table with me when mine was empty.

To the compassionate folks at the former Jewish Community Center in Far Rockaway known as the Hartman Y and, in particular,

Phil Goldberg (wherever he may be) for opening their doors and embracing a lost and lonely high school dropout. To the B'nai B'rith Youth Organization for helping me find the beginning of the path to success and the ability to lead.

To my dear friend Melanie Frank: without her friendship and early counsel in my life, my decisions could have been very different. Thanks to her dad, David, who talked to me about life, World War II, and his love of playing the drums, which I tried but could never learn to play. Also, thank you for putting up with the phone calls and trying to jog your memory when mine was fried.

I am always grateful to my current colleague Gail Becker who has put up with my moods but has held on to the roller-coaster ride over the last several years. To Robert Bashner, who is my partner at our law firm. When we first met thirty-five years ago, we connected immediately as we both had a parent with MS. Over the years our friendship turned to law partnership and his level of humanity and sense of awareness was always an asset.

I'd like to thank all those wonderful friends and colleagues who took the time to read and write some kind reviews and testimonials on the book. Thank you to (in no particular order) Harlan Schillinger, David Meerman Scott, Brian Mittman, Josh Goldstein, Mitch Jackson, John Fisher, Paula Cialella, Michael Samuel, Jennifer Quinn, Arnie Preminger, Gurpreet Singh, Christopher Nicolaysen, Ona Gritz, Jim Hacking, Michael Mogill, Ellen Feinstein, Ernest Mingione, and Seth Price.

To Bryan Kramer, the founder and instigator of the H2H (human-to-human) business movement for finding precious time to read my entire manuscript. I now know there are more of us "humans" out there than I imagined. Your heartfelt foreword and kind words moved me beyond description. Thank you.

To my social media and branding consultant Jennifer Quinn, otherwise known to her fans as JennyQ: thank you for your help walking me through the steps of getting my voice heard in an otherwise crowded space. Our relationship has grown, and I am highly grateful for regular Zoom meetings even when I'm not in the mood to "be seen" on Zoom. And yes, you are always right.

I will always be grateful to have the memory of my grandmother and my brother Cary. I miss them terribly and will never forget the laughs and good times. It was a gift to have you both in my life. As per your advice, my dear brother, I am still putting money in my 401(k).

Of course, thanks to all of you who have taken the time to read this book. I wish you much success, and I hope you now have some valuable tools to take with you on this amazing journey we call life.

ABOUT THE AUTHOR

At sixteen, Neal Goldstein dropped out of high school. It was the last in a long line of defeats, and it represented the acceptance of an inevitable fate.

Neal was an underprivileged boy, self-raised in a tumultuous home with an abusive father and a disabled mother who couldn't earn or fully take care of herself, let alone her three children. So Neal did the only thing he could think to do: quit dreaming of a future, get a job, and look after his mom as well as he could with his limited life skills.

Once Neal was able to find the genuine relationships he was searching for, he allowed himself to take the courageous steps of getting his high school equivalency diploma. It was only then that Neal felt the need to further his education and subsequently graduated from Queens College with a BA in political science and New York Law School where he earned his Juris Doctorate.

Neal Goldstein is a partner at the law firm of Goldstein and Bashner, a well-known and respected personal injury law firm on Long Island, New York.

He has in the past served in a leadership role at the New York State Academy of Trial Lawyers and was active with the Lawyers Division of the United Jewish Appeal.

Neal is most proud of the time he spent as chairman of the board of directors at the Friedberg JCC in Oceanside, New York. He has also been actively involved and asked to speak at the National Multiple Sclerosis Society on Long Island.

Recently Neal founded Coffee@3 Enterprises, which encompasses much of the philosophy in this book. Through this company, he has started a website, www.TruthInSuccess.com, where he shares his thoughts and opinions on building relationships genuinely and authentically.

Additionally, Neal is always available to speak at events and privately with individuals in both the private sector and not-for-profit sector about creating and strengthening relationships.

Neal lives with his wife Gina on Long Island. They have four children: Matt, Sari, Jessica, and Lana. He loves traveling, bicycle riding, and walking on the boardwalk in his hometown in his free time.